CLIMBING JACOB'S LADDER

*One Man's Journey
to Rediscover a Jewish
Spiritual Tradition*

Alan Morinis

Trumpeter
Boston & London
2007

Trumpeter Books
An imprint of Shambhala Publications, Inc.
Horticultural Hall
300 Massachusetts Avenue
Boston, Massachusetts 02115
www.shambhala.com

9 8 7 6 5 4 3 2 1

First Trumpeter Edition

Originally published in hardcover by Broadway Books

Printed in the United States of America
⊛ This edition is printed on acid-free paper that meets
the American National Standards Institute Z39.48 Standard.
Distributed in the United States by Random House, Inc.,
and in Canada by Random House of Canada Ltd

Library of Congress Cataloging-in-Publication Data
Morinis, E. Alan.
Climbing Jacob's ladder: one man's journey to rediscover a
Jewish spiritual tradition / Alan Morinis.—1st Shambhala ed.
p.   cm.
ISBN 978-1-59030-366-5 (alk. paper)
1. Spiritual life—Judaism. 2. Self-actualization
(Psychology)—Religious aspects—Judaism. 3. Jewish ethics.
4. Musar movement. 5. Morinis, E. Alan—Religion. I. Title.
BM723.M67 2007
296.8'32—dc22
2006102635

To the women in my life,
who have taught me love:
mother,
sisters,
wife,
daughters.

"Your deeds will bring

you near and

your deeds will put

you at a distance."

— MISHNAH,

EDUYOT 5:7

CONTENTS

CONTENTS

ACKNOWLEDGMENTS

This book has been aided by a divine spirit that was determined to see me be its agent, and for that relentless help, guidance, and sustenance, I am deeply grateful. It has been a gift, and I bow to the Giver.

So many people gave so generously to help me become a vessel to bring forward my learning in this ancient tradition. Above all, Rabbi Yechiel Yitzchok Perr, his wife Mrs. Shoshana Perr, their extended family, the community around the Yeshiva of Far Rockaway, Rabbi Hillel Goldberg, and Rabbi Daniel Nekritz opened their hearts and their homes to me, took me in, fed me, and saw me for who I am, and even then they didn't turn me away. Leonard Angel introduced me to Mussar, though he didn't mean to. The late Lama Geshey Dargey taught me a key lesson of spiritual practice—do it now, when you don't need it, so you'll have it when you do. Ruth Denison opened dharma doors that have never closed. Judy Kern helped immeasurably to turn my sprawling vision into a book.

Friends and kin served unfailingly to add pieces just when they were needed, and were stewards to this book as well as teachers to me: Hal Brown, Ellen Buchman, Peter Busby, Rabbi Rachel Cowan, Rabbi Nancy Flam, Cheri Forrester, Rabbi Tzvi Freeman, Rabbi Hillel Goelman, Daniel Goleman, Rahel Halabe, Steve Jones, David Kaetz, Shams Kairys, Michael Katz, Bonnie Klein, David Levine, Lorne Mallin, Sunanda Markus, Gabor Mate, Rabbi David Mivasair, Marilyn Morinis, Judy Moscowitz, Mr. and the late Mrs. Victor Pollack, Rochelle Rabinowicz, and William Irwin Thompson all made essential contributions. The members of the board of the Seva Foundation in my days with that conspiracy of love were the best fellow-travelers a pilgrim could ever hope for.

I owe a special debt of appreciation and gratitude to the group of people who first gathered with me to learn *The Duties of the Heart*, whose open hearts were a doorway through which I discovered the deep reservoir of wisdom that is the spiritual legacy of Mussar: Azima Buell, Fran Ritch, Barry Goodman, Anne Gorsuch, Gloria Levi, Hal Siden, and Helen Waldstein.

Parents' love can never be repaid. May the memories of Bessie Morinis (1910–2000) and David Morinis (1909–1993) be for a blessing.

Three women have shared the crucible of my life as this book was formed. The souls of my wife, Bev Spring, and our daughters Julia and Leora Morinis are there in every word. Lavish in their love, unstinting in their course corrections, a Godsend for their humor—companions, gifts, angels.

CLIMBING
JACOB'S
LADDER

INTRODUCTION

"The ear that hears the reproof of life will abide among the wise."

— BOOK OF PROVERBS

I have always known those large hazel eyes, and that off-center nose, and I was comfortably familiar with the person whose presence radiated steadily through the flesh of my face. But when my world suddenly came caving in around me, and darkness settled over my life, all my easy assumptions fled. For months I churned in pain and chaos, feeling that the blackness would reign forever. Gradually, though, I became aware that forgotten seeds that had lain dormant, maybe for generations, had started to germinate in the freshly turned soil of my life, and unknown roots had began to push up unexpected shoots through the darkness. Even now, as I look back over my entire life from this place where it all makes some sense, I can find few obvious signs that I would one day embark on a spiritual journey that would lead me deep into the byways of the Jewish world. But that is just what happened when I set out to reconstruct the pieces of my splintered life in a way that would be new and satisfying, and I took the first steps on the pilgrimage whose tale I am about to tell.

It was a business failure that knocked me flat and, in the wonderfully twisted way that life sometimes works, gave birth to my spiritual journey—back into history, across territories, and into worlds I hadn't even known existed. Pain and bitter turmoil propelled me to search, and what I found was Mussar—a little-known treasury of wisdom to guide the life of the soul that Jewish saints and seekers have accumulated in a thousand years of inquiry and experimentation. Through Mussar's teachings and practices, I have gained the insights that have transformed my life. My journey is far from over, but what I've seen to this point has been so compelling that I want to pause on the road for a moment to share some of what I've learned.

First, though, let's return to the places where those quiescent seeds were secretly planted, and the roots of my search first began to stretch themselves out within me.

I was born in Toronto to an unremarkable Jewish family consisting of my parents, two older sisters, and, for a time, even a dog. As the youngest child and the only boy, I enjoyed a nicely favored position in the family, as my sisters never tire of reminding me. My parents were both refugees from Europe who had arrived in Canada as children, sometime around 1920, their own parents having fled places where it was very difficult to be a Jew long before Hitler made it impossible.

My father held a number of jobs, at one time selling paper cups, at another representing a line of women's undergarments. My mother was a housewife. Once she married my father, she never worked another day outside the home. She also never drove a car, but she never really needed to, both because my father loved to drive and because the circle of her life never extended much beyond her family.

From before my earliest memories, we always lived in the same small house in a suburb where the streets were quiet enough for road hockey and no one ever got into any big trouble. During the long, cold winters, we built snow tunnels that suddenly collapsed when spring burst out one day, arriving on the backs of the robins and the hordes of butterflies that don't show up much in the city anymore.

Ours was a thoroughly Jewish home, although it was a Judaism defined more by gefilte fish and Milton Berle than by the Torah and the Talmud. We wore our Jewishness proudly, if cautiously, since the grievous lessons of history were still so fresh, but it was mostly a cultural and ethnic identity that had almost nothing to do with religion or spirituality. I can't remember my mother ever lighting the traditional Friday-night Sabbath candles, and my father didn't even own a *tallis*, the prayer shawl that is the most basic of paraphernalia for a Jewish man's religious observance. When I stood beside him at his own brother's funeral and the rabbi began reciting prayers, my father leaned toward me and whispered, "None of this baloney for me when I go." My parents, like many in their generation, willingly shucked off what they considered the superstitions and meaningless rituals of the Old Country in their quest for the progress, prosperity, and security that were finally possible for them in the New World.

Still, we were so Jewish. It was there in how we spoke, whom we knew, in the food my mother cooked, in the tunes my father hummed, and in the ethical standards that provided the lens through which other people were seen. My father was always

3

quick to let us know who was a *shmo,* a *shmendrick,* a *shlemiel,* or any of the many other terms Yiddish provides to pinpoint ethical failings with technical precision. To call someone a *mensch*— the ideal of human ethical perfection and uprightness—that was the highest praise he could convey.

Although not in the least observant, my parents seemed never to consider that their only son might not have a bar mitzvah, and so, soon after my twelfth birthday, I was sent for lessons. It was the same for all the boys in our Jewish neighborhood, and just like them, I submitted to becoming a man by learning to give a zombie-like recitation of a few Hebrew prayers and a passage of Torah, because we all had our eyes on the prize—a blowout party and more gifts than any of us could imagine. I still associate the tangy smell of freshly oiled leather with the gift I cherished most: a dazzling new pair of hockey gloves.

I went to high school just down the block, and although it was now the sixties and, on the news, we saw reports of cultural upheaval, only the faintest aftershocks reached our insulated suburban world. Some of the boys confronted the school administration over the ban they had imposed on sideburns; girls shortened their hemlines a millimeter at a time. Marijuana was introduced. There were rumors of sexual liberation.

I floated through those years in a state I can only describe as benign alienation. Nobody and nothing lit any fires under me, and I gave only as much to my schoolwork as was needed to ensure that I would graduate and move on to university without a hitch.

When that happened, I was suddenly hanging on to my hat as the little boat in which I had been gently drifting for so long got thrust headlong into a furious current. The force that swooped me up and away like that was William Irwin Thompson, an Irish cultural historian from California via MIT who taught a humanities course I took in my freshman year at York University. In his lectures, Thompson fired out words and ideas like no one I had ever encountered. Word jazz, he called it, and I came away from every one of his classes dizzy with discovery, my head whirling with ideas and inspiration. It was an intellectual magic carpet ride, and the boundaries of my little world were blasted wide open.

That alone would have made me ripe for an introduction to things I'd call spiritual, but the times they were a-changing, and while my course reading lists included Alan Watts, Teilhard de Chardin, and other spiritual thinkers, books by Ram Dass and Gurdjieff were being passed hand-to-hand among the students. I began to put together the outlines of the first map I'd ever had of an inner life, plotting ideas from the books I was reading right alongside what I was absorbing from sources all around me. Professor Thompson didn't make a big deal about it, but he also didn't hide the fact that he practiced yoga and meditation. I began to take yoga classes, too, though the stretches and bends didn't come very easily.

As an undergraduate, my intellectual appetite became so voracious that I wanted to learn everything, and so I took courses in science, philosophy, anthropology, art history—and even tried out for a modern dance course, though sadly I failed the audition. When it came time to graduate, my eclectic transcript divulged that I didn't have enough courses in any single discipline to qualify as a major. The university was very cooperative, though, and bent over backward to help me with this problem, since I had just done them the honor of being selected as a Rhodes Scholar.

Although I'd applied for that scholarship, I was so certain I wouldn't get it that when the phone call came, no one could have been more surprised than I was. I had all the necessary qualifications—grades, athletics, student government, social action—but my immigrant parents had so imbued me with the notion that prizes of this sort were intended for "them," never us, that I simply assumed I was not the sort of person Cecil Rhodes had had in mind when he established the award in his name. In addition, having gone my entire four undergraduate years without a single visit to the barber, my hair now reached my shoulders, which in 1971 was neither common nor generally accepted. As I approached the final interview, where I would face a committee made up of partners in major law firms, senior professors, and famous politicians, and chaired by the Chief Justice of the Supreme Court of Ontario, I was so convinced the sacrifice would be in vain that I couldn't bring myself to cut my hair.

If Professor Thompson had knocked down the mental partitions erected by my limited upbringing, Oxford leveled the ground for rebuilding. The barrage of ideas kept up, and now I had the added challenge of making my own way at this crossroads of the world. Having spent my entire life within a few miles of the place where I was born, I now found myself sitting in lectures and at dinner parties with students from every corner of the globe.

Studying anthropology at Oxford was half an exercise in learning and half simple veneration. British social anthropology had been born in those hallowed halls, where its founders were beatified with busts that encircled the small library at the Institute of Social Anthropology. One had already been installed for the last remaining grand old man, Sir Edward Evans-Pritchard—"E-P," as he was universally known. E-P could be seen from time to time ambling about assisted by a willowy young woman dressed all in white, but I assiduously avoided him. Who knew what frightening and demolishing fire this Titan breathed? Then, one night, as I worked late in the library, he walked in. There was only one other student there with me, and E-P glared at us for a moment from under his bushy gray eyebrows and above the top rim of his half-glasses before snarling, "What are you two doing in here trying to learn all these things I'm trying to forget?" Having lobbed that challenge at us like a stun-grenade, he then turned and disappeared.

At the time, I had no idea what he meant, or even if he were serious. Now, however, having myself abandoned the study of anthropology, I can understand his question, and sympathize with the plight of all social and cultural anthropologists, whose job it is to stand dispassionately on the sidelines while everyone around plunges head-first into the maelstrom of life. Standing aside to observe and analyze like that is alienating, and it can desiccate the soul.

I had gone to Oxford with a girlfriend from Toronto whom I loved too much to leave behind. Bev and I had met as freshmen at York and instantly fallen in love. She gave me her copy of *The Little Prince* and I reciprocated with Huxley's *The Doors of Perception*. We shared the joy of learning and the excitement of the late sixties, and when the opportunity came to live in Oxford, all expenses paid, there wasn't much to discuss.

Bev spent her time in Oxford riding her bicycle through the medieval lanes, baking bread, and reading. In reality she didn't have too much time on her hands because the terms at Oxford are only eight weeks long, followed by a six-week break, except in the summer when the break is sixteen weeks. We spent every "vac" traveling in England or Europe, and once venturing as far as Morocco.

We both studied yoga in the local gym, but while I continued to labor at loosening up stiff joints, Bev, naturally flexible, became a star pupil. In no time, she was biking around to teach classes of her own.

We got married in the summer between our two years at Oxford. Rhodes Scholars are not permitted to be married during their first year of residence, and so, when I had finished that first year and we were finally allowed to wed, the lifting of that restriction made it feel necessary to get on with what, until then, had been forbidden, and so we tied the knot.

My Oxford program required that I choose one of only three geographic areas to specialize in: peoples of the Nile Valley, the Amazon, or India. The simple fact that I had no real interest in tribal peoples pointed me to India, which, of course, suited me just fine. My interest in yoga and spirituality had already brought India clearly onto my radar screen. Now I did extra courses related to Indian society and culture, and Bev and I started learning Hindi.

As soon as we arrived in England, we bought a VW van, which I converted into a camper by cutting down and installing English antiques, including a drop-leaf table and an armoire. We traveled in the van between terms, and when my two years of study at Oxford were up, we set off overland to India. I had in mind that maybe I'd find a Ph.D. subject there. Then too, maybe we'd find a guru, or at least some deep and resonant teaching or practice. At the time, anything seemed possible, even driving through Iran, Afghanistan, and Pakistan, which we did without incident.

As it turned out, no sooner had we arrived in India than we fell into working with the World Health Organization, which was engaged in a global effort to eradicate smallpox, a disease that had ravaged India from the beginning of time. For two years we alternated stints of smallpox work with time spent seeking out the spiritual teaching we were looking for. We visited gurus and ashrams and spent time with Mother Teresa in the years before she was famous. We made pilgrimages to sacred shrines and sat by the banks of holy rivers. We hung out in temples and read Hindu and Buddhist scriptures. We continued to learn yoga, now from our teacher's teacher, B. K. S. Iyengar, and did silent Buddhist meditation retreats. Every day was an adventure. We knew that our work with the smallpox program was making a small but valuable contribution to the welfare of the world, and, at the same time, we were nourishing and nurturing our own inner growth.

We left India in 1976 and returned to Toronto. I got a job as a teaching assistant back at York University while Bev, who had been inspired by the smallpox program, applied to medical school, despite being a senior citizen at age twenty-six. By the end of that first year home, she had won her acceptance, and so we moved to Hamilton, Ontario. Once we had found an apartment and Bev settled into her studies, I returned to India to do research for my doctoral dissertation.

In our earlier travels in India we had been enthralled by its colorful and widespread tradition of pilgrimage, and I decided to make that my doctoral subject. It was a radical choice, because anthropologists normally study people as they live in their communities, which meant that pilgrimage, which pulls people out of their ordinary lives, had been little studied at that time. I traveled to various Hindu pilgrimage centers, where I mixed with saints and seekers, probing and trying to understand the devotion that moved millions of pious pilgrims to take to the road every year. It was academic research, but in truth, what kept luring me to India in the seventies, as it did so many of my generation, was the hope of tapping into that country's spiritual current in order to find meaning and direction in my own life. I was drawn to study pilgrims because, in my heart, I was a pilgrim too. What could I learn from these people who for centuries had prayed with their feet as they sought out the remote refuges of their gods? From my freshman year at York, through my time at Oxford, and on into India, I had been nurturing the seeds of a spiritual life, and I shared the pilgrims' hunger to grow and to blossom spiritually. I was inspired by their quest, and had never found anything in the Western religions that might even begin to satisfy my own inner needs.

After eight solid months of travel and research, I rejoined Bev in Hamilton, bought a new electric typewriter, and set about writing my thesis. But instead of the idyllic intellectual retreat I'd envisioned, this turned out to be the worst stretch of time we have ever faced as a couple. From the moment we met until I went to India on my own, every aspect of our lives had been lived in tandem. But during the last year our paths had diverged for the first time, and we were no longer sharing the same reality. One of the hardest adjustments we (really I) had to make was to the reversal of our relative status. Until then I had been El Primo, the Rhodes Scholar and Oxford doctoral candidate, while Bev had been my pleasant wife. Now, she was a physician-to-be, and that gave her primacy, especially since we were living on her turf. In that year after I rejoined Bev, people who met me for the first time were often surprised to learn that she and I had different last names, to which I would respond that I had decided to keep my own name. It didn't seem all that much of a joke to me.

We struggled to change and adapt to keep from going under, and our love proved strong enough to see us through the storm. I finished my dissertation, and in 1980 received my doctorate from Oxford, just as Bev finished her final exams and was about to enter her internship year. We both needed a fresh start, and we agreed that Vancouver might be just the place for that. I got a job teaching anthropology at Simon Fraser University, and Bev was accepted as an intern at a downtown Vancouver hospital.

In the years that followed, we gradually put down roots and made a home for ourselves. Bev set up a general practice, and I continued to teach. Three years later, the first of our daughters was born—our blonde Julia, followed in another three years by dark-haired Leora.

I taught at four universities during those years, but somehow none of them could quite measure up to my Oxford experience. I found myself growing increasingly disgruntled with the onerous burdens that academics in North America are expected to bear—administrative duties, committee work, and the huge volume of grading that goes hand-in-hand with large undergraduate classes. My first love was research, and I was still managing to write and publish quite a bit, but I was also beginning to feel the frustration of the anthropologist's position, which is so firmly rooted on the sidelines of life.

Friends we had made through the smallpox program in India had reconvened in North America to form a service organization called the Seva Foundation, and we joined the board. Even while still in India, one of the other board members had been an entrepreneur—buying up bales of homespun cotton for resale in America—and now he had stepped up the level of his financial activities to become a venture capitalist. At one point he formed a Canadian gold-mining company, and he needed a trustworthy Canadian to sit on the board of directors. Despite the fact that I knew less than nothing about finance and corporations, it seemed like an adventure, and I couldn't see much risk, so, sure, I said.

In only a matter of months my life had taken another sharp turn. By day I was still an anthropologist, teaching courses and writing about India and the life of the spirit, but by night I had become a financier. The company was traded publicly and the stock kept going up. People who knew people sent me checks in the mail. The amount of money flowing around was intoxicating, and it seemed all I had to do was scoop it up and redirect it to where we wanted it to go.

It appeared that I had been handed an extraordinary opportunity. If I worked hard and smart, I saw, I could make enough money in a short time to give up the university with all its balls and chains, and spend all my time reading, writing, and pursuing a life of the spirit.

At that time, Vancouver was the main capital market for mining ventures, and I could well have continued in that field, especially since I'd been on the board of a market high-flier. But I didn't feel any affinity to mining, and, in fact, was opposed to pillaging the earth for profit. So I began to wonder about other ventures that might allow me to fulfill my get-rich-find-God scheme while leaving my hands cleaner than they would be if I stayed in the world of mining. I made a switch, and none too soon, because the mining company went on to develop a gold mine in Colorado that turned out to be a gigantic environmental disaster.

It had been only four years since I completed my doctoral thesis on sacred journeys, and now I was preoccupied with finding an industrial field in which speculation and big payoffs were the norm. One soon showed up when I met a group of filmmakers who were looking for financing (as I now know filmmakers always are). I jumped at the chance, made myself president of the company (money doing the talking), and hatched a plan to expand the venture. The group I was with had been making high-end documentaries, and I grasped immediately that there was no money to be made in that field. I decided we should diversify into feature films, corporate multimedia, and animation, and within a couple of years our first feature, called *The Outside Chance of Maximilian Glick*, won the audience award at the Toronto Film Festival and was released to pretty good box-office. We'd also made a film starring Martin Sheen, and we'd produced a series of *Care Bear* cartoons.

I stuck to my plan and took the company public on the Toronto Stock Exchange. But soon after that, my inexperience caught up with me, and things began to get sticky. We weren't making enough money to interest the stockbrokers. Also, we hadn't penetrated that segment of the business where the risk is lowest and the returns to be skimmed are the highest, which is distribution. I didn't know enough about the industry to have realized that, and in any case it was production that really interested me. What had drawn me to filmmaking in the first place was the opportunity to actually produce a cultural product, which seemed to me much more satisfying than what I'd had to do in the hands-off role of anthropologist.

So our stock drifted lower. I was getting 7 A.M. phone calls at home from brokers asking why I wasn't supporting the stock. I, in turn, looked to my partners to deliver the successful productions we needed, but somehow they hadn't transformed themselves and were still the same documentary-minded producers they had been when we hooked up. They certainly gave no signs of being capable of performing the magic that would convert the dreams I had sold to the marketplace into reality. In the end, the company was taken over by a Los Angeles distribution company that could make better use of the public listing than I had.

I wasn't at all deflated by that outcome. Round One over, I said to myself. And I jumped right back into the ring and started my own film company, this time with no partners.

Life by this time had become all go-go and get-get, work and money having incrementally elbowed aside the spirituality and social action I had once believed to be so central to my life. My Buddhist meditation and yoga practices had slowly eroded until they finally disappeared entirely. Spiritual practice is no different from any other kind of daily exercise—skip one day, then find an excuse to skip another, and another, and finally your spiritual StairMaster is just gathering dust in a dark corner of your soul where the light never shines. Remnants of my old ideals remained, of course, especially in my own mind; in reality, however, the playing field of my daily life had come to be dominated by aspects of my character—ambition, vanity, ego—that had somehow remained completely untouched by the spiritual practice I had done so far. In and of themselves, these are not necessarily the forces of evil, but I hadn't yet done the work that would teach me how to control and guide them for the good.

Happily set up in my own company, I pursued my dream of making it rich. My former shareholders had inadvertently paid for my education in the industry, and now that I actually knew something about film production, my new company prospered. Our first feature film, called *Harmony Cats,* was nominated for twelve Genies, the Oscars of Canada, and was released theatrically in the U.S. before being sold to the HBO and Showtime networks. *Eye Level,* a TV miniseries we made, won a Silver Award at the New York Film Festival, while a Holocaust documentary called *Prisoner 88* won a Gold Plaque at the Chicago Film Festival.

Not only were my films winning awards, they were making money too, though not a lot. It was enough success to fuel my appetite for bigger things, but if the company were to grow, I would need more capital, and so I took in a well-heeled partner. Successes continued to roll my way, but I had my eye on still bigger game. More ambitious projects meant higher risk, and I embraced those risks as unavoidable. But then some disasters loomed in connection with a couple of large projects, and I became desperate to protect both my partner's investment and my own ego. By that time I had so lost my inner bearings that I recklessly tried to cover up the problems. The pressure I had brought upon myself was intense, and it led me to tell different stories to different people, foolishly hoping that "things would work out" before anyone discovered the truth. But, of course, in the end, I simply couldn't juggle fast enough, and with painful inevitability, one ball after another fell crashing to the ground. The company collapsed in a splattering of bile between my partner and myself and was soon wound up and out of business.

It could have been just another business failure, nothing so unusual in this fast-paced and risky world, but this fiasco nearly shattered me. Day after day, I was consumed by blackness. I spent hours immobilized on the couch, compulsively going over the details of my own actions. I had painted false pictures, made promises I should have known I couldn't keep, given people unrealistic projections, betrayed trust. Day after day, I cried with remorse. Bev and I had been married for twenty-four years by this time, through many ups and downs, and she would stand by me again. What sent me into a downward spiral was my own shock at realizing just how far I had strayed from what I'd always believed to be my true values, the sturdy, principled foundation upon which I had thought my life was based. What had happened to the favored son raised in that stable and ethical household in Toronto? Where was the yoga student, the meditator, the pilgrim striving so sincerely to live life up to his limits?

I was ashamed of myself, and, when I probed a little deeper, I was angry. How could I have been so stupid?

Near the end of Bev's and my first long stay in India, we paid a visit to the Tibetan settlement at Dharamsala, where the Dalai Lama had set up his center-in-exile, and took a course in Buddhist meditation. Sitting on the floor in that little Tibetan library, I heard many things from the teacher, most of them organized into long lists I could never quite remember—the thirteen attributes of something, the eight steps of something else. But one thing he said did stick with me: "Do spiritual practice now," he said, wagging a finger at us, "so that you'll have it when you need it." I was about twenty-five years old when I heard that lesson, and close to fifty when it came back to haunt me in my misery.

As a young seeker, I had been drawn to the light of Eastern religions, but even in those years there was always something in me that didn't quite fit, some hidden threshold I couldn't quite cross. Many of my friends took swami names or shaved their heads or donned robes, but I never did, I think because really deep down, I knew that just wasn't me. Despite those years at Oxford and all those months of Buddhist meditation and Hindu pilgrimages, when life whipped me around and stripped me bare and made me look myself right in the eye, I was still the little Jewish kid from the suburbs of Toronto.

My parents had escaped poverty and oppression in Europe to walk picket lines and earn a decent living in a new world. They were good people who, as far as I could tell, never perceived a trace of God anywhere in life. As a consequence, my sisters and I had been raised as secular, left-wing, activist Jews, with only a nod to religion and none at all to overt spirituality. But despite all that, when my soul cried out from the dark pit into which I had cast myself, and I began to clear away the cobwebs that had grown so thick over the spiritual pursuits of my youth, it was to the Jewish tradition that I turned. I had no real idea what I was looking for, or even where to look; I just hoped I'd be lucky (or blessed) enough to recognize it when I found it.

When our daughters were born, Bev and I had determined to raise them with a Jewish identity, and that decision had brought us into contact with practicing Jews. Now, when I started to reach out for Jewish wisdom, one of these friends lent me a book on Jewish spirituality that discussed every aspect of Jewish thought and practice from pre-biblical times to the present. I started reading it right from the beginning, and it was all interesting enough, though not exactly life-transforming. I'd had some intuition that the marvels of the Chassidic masters or the esoteric wisdom of the Kabbalah might set off sparks in me, but after reading those chapters I just kept going.

Then one evening I came to a chapter on the Mussar movement, founded in the mid-nineteenth century by a Lithuanian rabbi named Israel Salanter. One phrase in particular jumped out at me: "As long as one lives a life of calmness and tranquility in the service of God, it is clear that he is remote from true service . . ." What kind of spiritual teaching was this, whose ultimate goal was not serenity and inner peace? This was wisdom of a kind I'd never before encountered, and I wanted to know more about it.

As I continued my reading, a new (and very old) world opened up before me. I learned that Mussar is a path of spiritual practice that had developed within the Orthodox Jewish tradition over the last thousand years. It tells us that at our core we are all holy, and it shows us ways to change those qualities within us that obstruct the light of our holiness from shining through. It assures us that we are not condemned to live forever with every aspect of the personality we happen to have right now, but that we can make the changes that will set free the radiance of our inner light. And it provides a tool-bag of personal, introspective, and transformative practices that will lead us, step by step, along the path of purification and change.

This was the perfect message for me to receive at that despondent moment. Despite what I considered my "fall," I had never lost the sense that deep inside me, as in all of us, there was a still, deep pool of goodness. And what plagued me most about the things in me that had steered me so wrong was the realization that they were aspects of my character I simply hadn't done anything to deal with up to that point.

From the very beginning of my readings about Mussar, I became aware that the discipline filled in a missing piece of a puzzle for me. The Jewish tradition has been exceptionally precise at describing the ideal qualities to which we ought to aspire in our lives, but many of us who were exposed to Jewish practice in the late twentieth century felt like we were left largely to our own devices in finding the path that would lead us to those ideals. "Honor your parents." Okay, but what about my anger? "Be generous." But my hand doesn't open easily. Mussar is just that methodical path of individual transformative practice that can carry us from where we find ourselves today toward the ideal we seek. I had never encountered or even imagined that this sort of discipline had been developed within the stand-up/sit-down/recite-responsively religion I had seen in synagogue, though it was just such a path of practices and change I had sought and found in yoga and Buddhist meditation.

Mussar is not a discipline intended to be practiced in isolation, nor on the proverbial mountaintop. Yes, the practitioner is urged to separate him- or herself from the world, but only for periods of contemplative retreat. More value is actually placed on cultivating the inner resources that will allow us to carry on right in the midst of the bustling marketplace, but with the kind of strength and insight that will render us impervious to the powerful temptations society inevitably sends our way.

The main path of Mussar runs directly through everyday life, and that is where we are directed to look for our spiritual lessons—in how we treat our children, our neighbors, and ourselves. And because the work Mussar guides us to do is focused on features of our own personality, its practice has a place in every context. Dealing with the supermarket clerk or visiting with our family or even sitting down at our desk are all times when we might get by on habit and give ourselves over to negative impulses. But Mussar encourages us to see these moments as opportunities to sharpen our awareness and notch up the beauty and purity of our actions. In that way, everything we do in life becomes a part of the soul-work that will help to make us complete, or, some would say, whole, or—taking into account the divine dimension Mussar insists upon—even holy. But the Hebrew word *mussar* is now almost always translated into English as "ethics." And, at its simplest, the practice is indeed to lead an ethical life, which is exactly what I saw I had lost and needed to recover.

As I read, I learned more and more about the various strands of Mussar that had evolved through the centuries, and I grew to love what I had found. The characters of the Mussar world began to take on form and density until I felt myself being joined to those old men seeking truth and holiness in Spain or Lithuania in their distant time. I loved their dream of perfecting the world. I relished their holy heroics. It was balm to my sore heart, sustenance for my soul.

And yet there were problems. Mussar was conceived and is still put to use primarily to help Orthodox Jews abide by the demanding requirements of their observant way of life. While traditionally the study of Torah was restricted to men, the Mussar teachers insisted emphatically that Mussar's path of self-improvement was open to men and women equally. Whatever your gender, Jewish law says to give charity, for example—but what if you are miserly? Mussar can help. Jewish law says to love and care for your children, but what if you are almost always impatient with them? There are Mussar teachings and practices to help you overcome that, too. Mussar's job in the Orthodox world is to help people surmount whatever personal obstacles may be hindering them from living up to the traditional guidelines Judaism sets out as the path to a righteous life. Did this mean that if I wanted to study and practice Mussar I would also have to take on the full rigors of Orthodoxy? Or, could I—a Jew but not nearly so strictly observant in that way—nevertheless learn and profit from its teachings? Could Mussar, in effect, be of value in the modern, secular world? Even Rabbi Avraham Yoffen, one of the few Old World Mussar teachers to escape the Holocaust, had questioned that possibility. "How difficult it is to seize upon the ways of *The Duties of the Heart* or *The Path of the Just*," he wrote, referring to two of the great texts of the Mussar tradition, "where the greatest responsibility placed on a person is to undertake an internal reckoning, how hard it is to seize upon this way when the noise of New York obscures the sun itself."

As I sat alone in my study, reading the classic Mussar texts, these and an infinite number of other questions piled up in my mind, with no way of being resolved. And so it eventually began to dawn on me that I was reaching the limits of what I could learn on my own. I needed a teacher to guide me, but how and where would I find one? There was no listing for Mussar Teachers in my copy of the Yellow Pages, and even a search through the various course offerings in college-level Jewish Studies programs, at Jewish spiritual retreat centers, and at summer learning programs yielded no answers to my dilemma. Friends and colleagues more knowledgeable than I was hadn't even heard of Mussar, or, if they had, they thought it was a practice that might have long since died out. Finally, having exhausted all my leads, I began to think they could be right. Dozens of Mussar teachers and thousands of its students had, after all, been devoured in the flames of the Holocaust.

Then a friend brought me a book he had found on a visit to New York. It was a small volume called *Novarodok,* by Meir Levin, which recorded some of the teachings and history of one of the branches that had emerged in the Mussar movement in the late nineteenth century. Printed at the front were two letters from rabbis attesting to the authenticity and significance of the book. Both letters had been reproduced just as they were received, complete with letterheads. The telephone numbers on the letterheads were tiny but still legible, and I decided to phone the authors of these approbations.

The first rabbi received me cordially but didn't seem to understand what I was after. He suggested I take courses at a seminary for people coming to the observant life for the first time. That wasn't what I was looking for, and so I went on to call the writer of the second letter, Rabbi Yechiel Yitzchok Perr, who, I could see from the letterhead, was the head of a yeshiva in Far Rockaway, on Long Island in New York. Our conversation was brief. He asked few questions and seemed totally unsuspicious of my uninvited approach. Twice in the course of my explaining the search that had brought me to call him, he said, "That's so inspiring!" And I felt that he meant it. I asked if I could come to meet him; then, having never had the slightest exposure either to

Orthodox Judaism or to a yeshiva, and with virtually no idea of what I was getting myself into, I cautiously suggested that I might come for a very brief visit sometime soon and, if that worked out, return another time. He agreed, and I still remember how elated I felt.

It is my good fortune that both my wife and my children love me enough to have supported me on this journey. I know they sometimes thought I was going off the deep end. My children took to teasing me, calling me "Chassy," as in Chassidic, that almost cult-like branch of devotional Judaism. To me, this was an indication that they didn't want me to turn into someone who was unrecognizable to them. And even Rabbi Perr at one point cautioned me not to "go faster than your wife." But my family also knew how deep was the pit into which I had fallen, and as time went on they appreciated the fact that Mussar was genuinely providing me with a set of handholds I could use to pull myself out. It is also a testimony to Mussar that my study and practice haven't taken me away from them but have, on the contrary, brought more love and understanding into our household.

In this book, I hope to pass along some of the lessons and practices I have learned in the course of my conversations with Rabbi Perr. In the three years since my initial visit, I have spent many hours with him, sometimes staying at the yeshiva for up to a month at a time. But for our purposes I have taken the liberty of turning each chapter into a specific "conversation" with the intent of clarifying or imparting a particular Mussar lesson or practice. In no way does this distort or change what he told or taught me, but I hope it will allow you, the reader, to share in my journey without having to travel the many byways, dead ends, and wrong roads I took along the way. My lessons certainly aren't finished—perhaps they never will be—but what I have learned so far has provided me with just the set of wise signposts I have needed in my life, and my intent here is to illuminate those signposts insofar as I am able, so that others can see them as well.

The classic texts of the Mussar tradition often name their chapters "gates," conveying the idea that each one will swing open to a new subject, as a gate does to the next field. I like this image, and so I have adopted the term "gate" to name my chapters as well. In so doing, I also intend to pay honor to the tradition of Mussar teaching and learning. And, because Mussar is all about practice and growth, at the end of each chapter I have included an exercise or practical method from the Mussar tradition that you can apply in your own daily life. I have called these sections "Opening the Gate."

The biblical story of the Patriarch Jacob tells of his traveling out into the desert, where he lay his head on a rock and had a dream. In his dream he saw a ladder with its base planted firmly in the earth and its top reaching into heaven. Angels were ascending and descending the ladder. This appears to me as a good image for the spiritual life. Our feet touch the earth because we are undeniably human and should have no illusions that our spirituality will separate us from all the beauty and suffering our humanity brings. But, without negating for an instant the realities of our humanness, each of us is also endowed with the gift of spirit, so that we can climb the ladder of the soul to reach its heavenly heights.

"How holy is this place," says Jacob. "The Lord is here and I didn't realize. This is surely the gate of heaven."

Jacob wasn't referring to some special faraway place or an exalted shrine when he recognized that he was standing at the gate of heaven. It's right here, he said, in this totally unremarkable place, *now that I realize it*. When consciousness awakens to the realization that life is a journey of the soul, and embraces life just as it is, right here, then we discover that, right now, we ourselves are standing at the foot of Jacob's ladder. The steps are there before us, waiting to be climbed.

This explains why seekers on Mussar's way are called the *b'nei aliyah*, which means "members of the fellowship of the ascent." This fellowship has no membership cards. There is no website. Entrance is based solely on one criterion: that you make the effort to rise up. The tales of the journey left for us by those who have gone before show us the way, and provide us with a map and also techniques to help us make the climb of our lives. At the top is a life of holiness, and Mussar teaches that it is possible for us to reach that pinnacle.

Whether or not any of us is ever so blessed, what I have learned thus far is that the journey, in and of itself, is transformative. My hope is that you, too, will find in the learning and practices I have so far discovered along Mussar's path something that will help you find ways to direct and enrich your own life.

CHAPTER ONE

THE GATE OF STARTING OUT

In a classic Jewish story, a student tells his friend that he is going to study with a teacher. "What do you hope to learn?" his friend asks him. "I want to see how he ties his shoes," he answers.

The streets of New York streamed with people, and the stairs to the subway were like a giant drain sucking up the wash of a human rainstorm. I boarded a train at Penn Station on my way to my first meeting with Rabbi Yechiel Yitzchok Perr at his yeshiva in the unlikely mecca of Far Rockaway, on Long Island. It was a warm day in the early spring of 1999, and I had already traveled a long way.

I had spent the night with a friend in Manhattan, having arrived the day before after a five-hour flight from my hometown of Vancouver, British Columbia. I had hugged my girls good-bye when they went off to school in the morning, and my wife had driven me to the airport. Our farewells were subdued. I could feel that my family was happy for me as I finally stepped out on this journey that had been in the making for two years, and yet there was more than a touch of apprehension in the air as well. None of us, including me, really knew where I was going or what I was about to find there. Would I come back as the dad and husband they loved, or different in ways that might drive wedges into our close relationships?

It had been an even longer journey emotionally from the brutal moment of awakening I had suffered two years before. Little by little my heart had healed, helped along by the reading and learning I was doing in the classic texts of the Mussar tradition. At first the dense and archaic philosophical language in these centuries-old books had been a barrier to me, but in time I had developed ways to connect myself to their wisdom. When a writer said "men," for example, I would think "people." When he talked about "sin," I would take this to mean ignorant or mistaken actions that led to suffering. In this way, I had read and reread, reinterpreted, and come up with images and metaphors that were meaningful to me while still remaining true to the core of their insights. Although it was the brilliance of these insights that had drawn me deeper into Mussar, I had now come to the point where I needed more than books. The theory was great, but it appeared to me like still-life paintings of a distant land. I needed to see how the wisdom of Mussar translated into the living qualities of someone who walked its path, and I hoped to find that person in Rabbi Perr.

On the flight and again on the train, I nervously ran through all the preparations I had made. I knew I was guaranteed to be as much of an "odd duck" in the regimented yeshiva environment as a Canada goose among penguins, but still, I had tried to remember to bring all the special things I knew I would need. I had brought a hat, because men in Orthodox communities wear hats—though I knew theirs would be black and mine was sort of grayish, which made me wonder if, instead of helping me "blend in," it would only point up just how much of an alien I was in their world. I had packed my prayer shawl, my *tallis*, and borrowed *tefillin*, the little black leather boxes with thongs that observant men strap on daily, which I had put on a grand total of twice in my life. I expected that the men would all have beards, though I had decided not to grow one myself. Even if they were all bearded, I had told myself, I wasn't on this journey to *become* one of them, certainly not before I had even set foot among them. I was on my way to deepen my learning of Mussar, and when I remembered that fact, a bright swell of happiness rolled through me. But bang behind it came a wave of hot anxiety, as the reality of what I was doing actually hit home. I'd never even laid eyes on a yeshiva in my life, and now I was on my way to meet the senior rabbi of one on his own turf.

As the train rocked me closer to that first meeting, I wondered what Rabbi Perr would be like. I had had only that first cold-call conversation with him and then one other to set the date and time of my visit, so I really had no clues to go on. Would he be warm and friendly or standoffish and detached? Joyous or austere? Approachable or remote? And I also wondered—and worried—how he would welcome an outsider like me. Would he be the kind of person to judge me on my clean-shaven cheeks and funny hat, or would he focus at a deeper level to see me as just another soul out on God's road?

By this time I had already come to see myself as a soul. That's one of the first things any student of Mussar needs to understand

and acknowledge, deeply and clearly. Each of us is a soul. Mostly we have been told that we "have" a soul, but that's not the same thing. To have a soul would indicate that we are primarily an ego or a personality that in some way "possesses" a soul. It's an early step on the path of Mussar to unlearn that linguistic misconception and to realize that our essence *is* the soul and that all aspects of ego and personality flow from that essence. At its core the soul is pure, but habits, tendencies, and imbalances often obscure some of that inner light. The Mussar discipline was devised to help us correct whatever shortcomings may be preventing the light of our soul from shining through.

At last the train pulled into the Lawrence station, where I'd been told to get off, and I knew all my questions would be answered soon enough. A short taxi ride through tree-lined suburban streets took me to the squat, red-brick building that housed the yeshiva. For a moment I stood outside and stared at the bunkerlike facade, hoping to make some connection between this ordinary, American-looking place and the ancient world of Mussar I knew from books. As I stood there, all the nervousness and uncertainty I had been feeling suddenly welled up into a tidal wave of anxiety that washed over me and left me feeling drained and totally unprepared for this meeting. In that moment, like a little kid being ushered toward his first day at a new school, I had the overwhelming urge simply to turn and flee. Except, I reminded myself, no one was making me come here. I had made the journey to the bottom of these stairs only because I really wanted to be here, maybe even needed to be. And so, with hat on head and trepidation in hand, I walked up the steps and pushed open the door to find myself in a long, narrow hallway teeming with boys in black *yarmulkes* rushing, jostling, and yelling at one another.

The door labeled OFFICE was right there, so I quickly made for refuge and found myself in a tiny room with a woman sitting at a desk. I asked for Rabbi Perr, and she wordlessly nodded over her shoulder toward another short hallway. Students and bearded teachers in ties and dark suits popped in and out of the several offices that opened onto the narrow passage. At the end I came to a door that stood partially ajar and was marked with a plaque that read ROSH YESHIVA, "head of the yeshiva." My way was blocked by a man leaning through the opening and talking to the person inside. Finally he left, and I poked my head into the small room.

Directly across from me sat a man whom I judged to be in his sixties wearing a round-brimmed black hat that tilted backward when he raised his head to look at me. His neck, collar, and the upper half of his shirt were hidden by a thick, wiry, graying beard, and as he rose to greet me the tails of his black frock coat fell to the backs of his knees. He presented an imposing, even patriarchal figure, though his eyes, peering out between the brim of his hat and the top of his beard, were large, dark, and warm.

I introduced myself and he responded enthusiastically "Welcome!"

Slowly he crossed to me. Then, taking my hand in both of his, those soft eyes gazing directly into mine, he asked, "May I give you a kiss?"

A kiss! I had thought that, in my anxiety, I'd rehearsed every possible greeting I might conceivably receive from this man, but a kiss hadn't even crossed my mind. I must have given some sign of consent, however, because he cupped my face in his

31

hands and, through the rasp of his beard, I felt his warm lips on my cheek. In that moment, relief coursed through my entire body.

He ushered me to a chair, then stuck his head out the door and nabbed a student whom he directed to get me a cup of coffee and a bagel. Settling back into his own chair, he took a deep breath, and said, "So, you are here."

Rabbi Perr inquired about my trip, my family, and my well-being before beginning to tell me something about himself and his yeshiva. He'd been born to an Orthodox family in Queens, where his father, also a rabbi, had served a small congregation. Surprising to me, he had attended a secular public kindergarten before starting the training in traditional Jewish learning that had led to his founding this yeshiva in 1969. Describing what he considered his role in guiding the lives of his charges, he quoted Rabbi Israel Salanter, who had started the Mussar movement in Eastern Europe in the nineteenth century: "Teaching children," he said, "is like holding a bird. You have to hold firmly enough that they don't fly away, but not so tightly that you crush them." Hearing that, I relaxed a little more, since I figured the dictum applied to me, too.

As we continued to talk, we were interrupted by a faint tapping at the door. A teenage boy warily stuck his head into the office. He was tall, thin, awkward, with short-cropped red hair that resolved into twirling earlocks that were tucked behind his ears.

"Come in, Reuven," Rabbi Perr said, motioning him forward with his hand.

Silently, the boy approached and timidly handed over what appeared to be a couple of dollar bills.

The rabbi thanked him with apparent enthusiasm, looked at the bills for a moment, then handed them back. "Here, you take it. Enjoy it."

The boy's face flushed bright enough to raise the temperature in the room by several degrees, then he gingerly took the money, and, mumbling something unintelligible to me, backed out the door.

I looked at Rabbi Perr quizzically, and with a small smile on his lips, he explained. "About a year ago, I sent that boy to run an errand for me. He did it, but he forgot to bring me the change. I saw him about a week later and reminded him, but before he could bring me the money, he went off to study in Israel for the rest of the year. He came back just a few days ago, and I ran into him. 'Reuven,' I said, 'how are you, and how was Israel? And what about my change?' So now he's given it to me, and I've made my point. Of course, I had to give him back the money to show him it wasn't really the two dollars I was interested in. Two dollars, two hundred dollars, two thousand dollars, the teaching is about character, not quantity."

Here it was, my first experience of Mussar in action. The rabbi's point to the boy was that even the most mundane and trivial detail can help us to make critical distinctions—between this and that, mine and yours, right and wrong. This kind of training and practice for spiritual perfection is at the core of Mussar, which is all about increasing the purity of our actions, one baby step at a time, because paying attention and acting well in small ways is how we move ourselves higher and higher toward our potential, and also prepare for life's bigger tests.

As I was still reflecting on this living lesson in Mussar, Rabbi Perr pulled me back with a question.

"You know the story of Abraham's sacrifice of his son Isaac?" he asked.

When I indicated that I did, he went on. "I've been thinking about that story lately. After Abraham has Isaac up on the altar, he is told by the angel not to bring the knife to the boy. What's going through his mind at that moment? He was told to sacrifice Isaac, but now he has to wonder, 'If I'm not here to sacrifice my son after all, then what am I here for?' "

He paused, his sparkling eyes fixed on mine, before probing deeper. "That's the question, isn't it? 'What am I here for?' "

Silently, he let me recall Abraham, who had thought he was doing God's bidding until he was told not to go ahead. At that point, he had to wonder, "What does God really want from me?" Rabbi Perr was using this well-known biblical story to introduce a new perspective on the similar question I'd been asking myself for the last two years. If my purpose was not to succeed in worldly ways and gratify my own ego, then just exactly what was I here in life to do? Though we had just begun to talk, and so at this point he really knew nothing about me or my personal history, it wasn't psychic powers that led him to score this direct hit on the very issue that had brought me to him. What I was asking of life and why I had come to him were all familiar territory, because my ailments were not just my own; they were maladies of the modern age, and he had seen them time and time again. But what did he have to say to this?

"Technology," he continued, "has provided us with an easier life than humanity has ever known. Now we have the opportunity and the privilege to step back, as Abraham did, and ask, 'What am I here for?' because there comes a point when the accumulation of more 'things' does not satisfy us."

Not material goods but spiritual goods, that's what we're here for. He was about to go on when the phone rang and we were interrupted again, giving me a few minutes to think about what he had just said, and how true it was for me.

The call, I quickly gathered, was from someone inquiring about a boy who was being considered as a potential marriage partner for his or her daughter.

"He's a good boy. You don't need to ask any more," Rabbi Perr assured the caller. He seemed suddenly weary.

Well, it wasn't *his* daughter, and the concerned parent apparently had plenty more to ask. As the conversation continued, I took the opportunity to look around the room. The walls of his office were covered in shiny, utilitarian wood-grained paneling. On either side of the desk stood two tall cases filled with books, all of them in Hebrew. Behind me, a couple of tables were piled high with the detritus of a scholarly life: books, papers, food containers, and a mousetrap, all frosted with a thick coating of dust. A spool of cable sat on the floor. A dusty black jacket and three black umbrellas hung from a metal coat rack. Above it, on a shelf, sat a single boot and a crumpled hat, also gray with dust.

Through the open window I could see and hear girders being swung into place for a new wing that was being added to the yeshiva. Perhaps that accounted for at least some of the dust.

My eyes returned to Rabbi Perr, still ensnared on the phone. He was taller than I had imagined. The hat sitting firmly on his head added a good six inches to his height, but even without that boost it seemed he was taller than me, and I stand six feet one. Adding in his long, peppery beard, everything attached to his head extended a total of about two feet, from the tip of hat to the last straggling hairs of beard. Near the middle, between the inert

35

mass of beard and the black capital of his hat, lived a pair of vibrant dark eyes, heavy-lidded and surmounted by thick eyebrows, but peering out from the depths of their forest cover with a calm and a clarity that instantly earned trust.

Rabbi Perr shifted in his chair and turned slightly away from me, and now I listened to his voice. It was deep and masculine, resonating with the tones of Eastern Europe and overwritten with the inflection of nasal New York. To me it sounded comforting and familiar, and I realized it was not only his eyes but also this voice that had immediately drawn me to him. In the way he said *Toirah* instead of Torah, *Shabbos* instead of Shabbat, I could hear echoes of my own Yiddish-speaking father. It was the perfect accent for telling a story.

Finally, with a deep sigh of relief, the rabbi hung up the phone, slapped his hands on the arms of his chair, and said, "Come, let's go to lunch. You'll meet my wife."

Rabbi Perr led as we walked the few blocks to his home, his broad, black-clad shoulders falling in a slight stoop. I was just happy to be breathing the fresh spring air after the old-socks mustiness of the yeshiva.

In a very short time, he led me around the back of an unassuming brick house to enter what once must have been the sunroom. Now the walls were lined from floor to ceiling with books, many of which were extraordinarily tall, exotic-looking leatherbound volumes dressed in covers of rich purple, wine, blue, and black, their spines stamped in gold leaf with Hebrew letters. Set against one wall was a short ladder for reaching the highest shelves.

No sooner had we come through the door than Mrs. Perr appeared. I was sufficiently aware of Orthodox custom to know that I shouldn't extend my hand to her. She wouldn't have taken it, I was sure, and it would have been an awkward moment. Instead, I exclaimed truthfully how much she looked like my wife. Both of them stand no more than five feet, but it was the similarity of their hair that was so startling. Mrs. Perr's was not only the same tawny shade of red but also about the same length and with the same bouncy curl as my wife's.

I was going on and on about this until a sudden thought thundered through my brain. Didn't Orthodox women wear wigs? It wasn't even her own hair I had been going on and on about! All the anxiety that had slowly ebbed from me in Rabbi Perr's congenial presence came roaring back, and my eyes now burned holes in the toes of my shoes. I was only saved when Mrs. Perr graciously invited us to the table.

This was only the first of many humbling gaffes I would make as I stumbled my way along the convoluted paths of this foreign culture. Orthodoxy has its own grammar, and there was no hiding the fact that I hadn't yet learned the language.

Mrs. Perr sat with us for lunch, but she continually kept an eye on our needs and was quick to jump up and provide whatever seemed called for. She joined fully in our conversation, which wasn't surprising considering that the main topic was her father, Rabbi Yehudah Leib Nekritz. I learned that at the time of the first World War, when he was a student in a Mussar yeshiva in Russia, he had escaped into Poland, where he settled. Then, when World War II broke out, the Russians invaded eastern Poland and exiled him and his family—including the young Mrs. Perr-to-be—to Siberia. At the time it seemed a fate worse than death, but it proved to be the surprising ticket to survival, because soon after that the Nazis rolled into Poland and deported to concentration camps all those whom the Nekritz family had left behind.

After the war, the family came to Brooklyn, where they joined Mrs. Perr's maternal grandparents, who had preceded them. Her grandfather, Rabbi Avraham Yoffen, had been a direct disciple (and son-in-law!) of one of the great Mussar masters of the nineteenth century, Rabbi Yosef Yozel Hurvitz, the Alter (Elder) of Novarodock. It was Rabbi Yoffen who first taught Mussar to Rabbi Perr, and who ordained him a rabbi.

Mrs. Perr talked expressively about her experiences in Siberia. "We lived in a little hut, so small a person couldn't stand up in it. My father, like all the exiles, was put to work cutting trees. I can remember that the cold was so bitter he would stuff straw into his thin boots to try to keep warm. When he returned home at the end of each day, he would tell me that he had cut down the biggest tree he could find in the forest. I was always amazed." She paused and set down her fork. "And that became a very formative story for me, and it influenced me, so that every time I was faced with a difficult challenge, I would think of my father out in the forest cutting down the biggest tree."

Rabbi Perr then added, "It was only years after hearing this story that I realized it couldn't possibly have been true."

I noticed Mrs. Perr stiffening and fidgeting, and he turned to face her directly.

"No, it couldn't possibly be true. No one could have survived if they set themselves to chopping down the biggest tree. It would take too much energy. They didn't have the calories to do more than just survive."

To which Mrs. Perr reiterated, "But it was a very formative story for me."

At which Rabbi Perr threw in: "A legend."

And she ended it with, "Okay, a legend. But it told me to face and take on what was there for me."

I lapped up this Mussar teaching. Rabbi Nekritz had used his experience in Siberia as raw material to convey to his daughter an ethic for living, and he had succeeded. Events of his life had been reworked to provide Mussar guidance.

When we returned to the yeshiva after lunch, afternoon prayers had already begun. The prayer hall, called the *Beis Medrash*, was filled with rows of narrow tables at which stood about two hundred boys, all of them dressed uniformly in dark pants, white tieless shirts open at the neck, dark jackets, and black felt hats. Rabbi Perr joined the adult men occupying a front row of tables set on either side of the cabinet that housed the Torah scroll, and I took an empty place off to the side, where I hoped to be inconspicuous. The room was already abuzz with prayer, so I picked up a prayer book and sidled discreetly over to the person beside me, trying to see what page we were on. The book was all in Hebrew, even the page numbers, and so I took an estimate of how deep into the book he was, and opened to about the same place.

At first it seemed to me that everyone was bobbing and weaving as one. Gradually, however, I could discern that each of them was actually off on his own, running through the prayers at his own pace. One might rock rhythmically back and forth while another swiveled from side to side. A couple in front of me remained seated and engrossed in a conversation that lasted throughout the entire brief service. At various intervals, the leader would loudly and slowly intone the last phrases of a prayer, pulling everyone into unison for a teetering instant before each roared off again on his own for the next of the prayers.

As I glanced around me, I couldn't help noticing how much this lack of unison was reflected in the disorder of the room itself. Coats were flung across tables, books piled on chairs, bags were dropped on the floor, and papers spilled from shelves. It struck me that if this room were to come alive as a person, its shoelaces would be undone and its shirttails flapping. I realized this probably had something to do with the fact that it was a room filled with teenage boys, but I noted too how different were the bustle, noise, and chaos from anything I had encountered in the meditation centers I had visited, where a carefully crafted order and beauty were meant to mirror the inner tranquility and perfection sought by their students. Still, this room had its own homey and appealing qualities. It was clearly a place where these people felt comfortable; it was as familiar to them as a workshop to its craftsmen.

Just as in the European yeshivas I had read about, the prayer hall in Far Rockaway stands at the physical and spiritual center of the institution and is the place where the three obligatory periods of prayer take place each day. It is also here that every student devotes many hours each day to traditional Jewish learning. But the adult men of the community who live within walking distance also gather here to pray and to study. The only times I saw women attending services were on the Sabbath and at festivals, when they occupy their own room, separated from the *Beis Medrash* and the men by a curtain.

Yeshivas come in many forms, ranging from highly organized, well-endowed educational centers that are much like colleges to informal but regular gatherings of a handful of scholars and students who study together. Rabbi Perr's yeshiva is definitely institutional. It has all the accoutrements you'd expect in any well-equipped American high school, and its new building is being erected to handle the need for more space. Current registration stands at more than two hundred students who range in age from fourteen to twenty-two and are mostly drawn from the New York area, although some come from as far away as Europe.

As I stood among them that first day, listening to their loud, indistinct devotions, punctuated from time to time by Rabbi Perr's chant rising in poignant melody above the rest, I tried as best I could to follow along in my prayer book. But this crowd raced at Formula One speeds, and my Hebrew skills, although they had improved with my recent studies, barely allowed me to keep my finger at the right point in the text all the way to the end. Despite my preoccupation with ensuring I didn't stumble and fall flat over my ignorance of things that any eight-year-old boy ought to know (as Bev had once done when, on a visit to a saintly leader in India, she innocently reached out toward him only to see him recoil at the threat of her touch and to hear an audible gasp from all around), I retained enough presence of mind to appreciate the remarkable scene around me—and to secretly enjoy the fact that, limping though I might be, I was actually a participant too. Something inside me that had grown musty and cobwebbed came curiously alive in that place, stirred by the chanting that filled the room. Jumping to stand when everyone else did, and listening to the ancient melodies and rhythms, it seemed as if there were a tune being sung directly to me that filtered out between the lines of their chant, something that gave me an intuition of home, even though, in so many ways, this was as alien a place as I had ever visited. In the line of a man's nose or the curve of a boy's cheek, I detected a hint of the legions that had come before, who had shared in these same ancient, plaintive melodies that now swirled around the room. I smiled to myself, then, savoring for a moment the realization that I had actually arrived.

When it was over, I was relieved to have got through the whole twenty-minute service without making any embarrassing bloopers—none that I was aware of, anyway.

Directly after prayers, a small group of boys drew up chairs around Rabbi Perr, who was about to give his daily Mussar discourse, which is technically termed a *shmuess* though everyone says it just like '*shmooze*,' that wonderful Yiddish word that describes a particularly informal kind of talking. *Shmooze* is to "talk" as *stroll* is to "walk." Calling it a *shmooze* seems to have given this daily class a license to roam, so that whatever the subject, it is explored in a leisurely and genial fashion.

The *shmooze* is not part of the formal yeshiva curriculum. "If I made it compulsory, they would all come," Rabbi Perr told me. "I don't want that. I only want the ones who want to be here." As a rule, only the senior students, about twenty in number, are permitted to attend the *shmooze*. That day, I became the newest student. The rabbi patted an empty chair at his side to indicate that I should sit. Then a book was set in front of me. All in Hebrew. I could follow the text but couldn't translate. Rabbi Perr, however, conducted the *shmooze* in English.

First he read a line from the text: " 'Do not place a stumbling block before a blind man.' " Then he made a Mussar lesson of this teaching by comparing a stumbling block to bad advice. "Giving bad advice is like tripping a blind man," he declared. "You have to look inside yourself with honesty to see if you have any self-interest in the advice you're giving." Taking another example from the text, he asked, "Are you encouraging someone to sell his farm in order to buy a donkey?" Then he translated that analogy into terms his students would understand. "That's like advising someone to give up their profitable business and buy a taxi. Would you suggest that only to give yourself the opportunity to buy the land or the business? It's obvious that you shouldn't do that," he concluded.

The boys around me were listening intently, some were even taking notes. This was the transmission of a lesson in living—an elder sharing what he had learned in his own life in order to introduce younger souls to the depths of their inherited tradition. And it struck me that this kind of teaching is as ancient as human culture, and that it rarely happens anymore in our modern and spiritually impoverished world.

Rabbi Perr's *shmooze* set off no fireworks that day. No one swooned. No one leaped to his feet and yelled "Eureka!" or the Hebrew or Yiddish equivalent. But every day he would offer another lesson, laying another brick that would help his students build a solid foundation for their lives.

As he finished and eased his large frame from the chair, the students respectfully got to their feet. Heading for the door, Rabbi Perr carved a path among them, and I followed in his broad wake as he led the way back to his office.

As he settled himself behind his desk he sighed, but not unhappily. He took off his hat, and found a place for it on top of the mound on his desk, settled back in his chair, and then remarked: "I don't expect they will remember anything I have taught them." He went right on to explain. "It's like bees. First, they have to build the honeycomb out of wax. Only later do they collect the pollen and bring it to the hive and make honey that they fill into the honeycomb. I'm building their honeycomb. Later in life, when they collect experiences, they will have where to put them."

It was now late afternoon and I still hadn't asked the question that had been on my mind for so long, and that had suddenly gained new urgency in the face of my first exposure to the reality of this tightly orchestrated ritual world. Did the study of Mussar inevitably mean that one had to follow the rigors of Orthodoxy, or could it be useful to people like me, who do not live according to Orthodox rules but who, nevertheless, believe that there are good directions for living in traditional sources such as the Bible?

He listened to my question, and then conceded, "Ah, here we are caught. Even for a person who strictly follows the Torah, there are many instances where judgment is required." He paused for a breath and stood up. He walked around from behind his desk and sat down again in the chair right beside me.

"Let me tell you a story," he said, leaning over to be close to me. "Once there was a man in a concentration camp whose son had just been grabbed and taken to the pen where they kept the people who were going to be gassed. The man was frantic. He found the only rabbi in the camp and asked him, 'Rabbi, my son is to be gassed. All my time here I have hidden a little piece of gold. I could bribe the guard to release my son, but I know they will then grab another person to make up their numbers. Is this permitted?' "

Rabbi Perr paused to ensure that I had time to grasp what a difficult question and dilemma had been presented. I thought, too, how remarkable it was that even with the life of his son in the balance, this faithful man sought out the guidance of tradition. Where was right?

Then in a quiet voice, Rabbi Perr went on. "The rabbi thought and thought, and finally answered, 'I don't know. I know that it is not permitted to endanger someone else to save yourself, but that's not what you're asking. In this case, when it is to save someone other than yourself, I just don't know.' "

Rabbi Perr had been nudging my elbow with his hand as he made his points. Now he put his large hand on my forearm and squeezed.

"The man was stunned for a moment, then he said, 'You are the only rabbi in this entire camp, and you don't know the answer. What does this mean? Does God want me to decide for myself?' "

Rabbi Perr let this notion sink in for a second, then concluded, "Yes, this is just what I think we have to do. Mussar helps prepare you to make such choices, but it is through maturity, judgment, and learning from experience that you develop a sense that you are indeed being honest with yourself, and about yourself. You develop confidence in your own honesty."

He had not answered my question directly, but still his answer amazed me. As an Orthodox rabbi, his traditional role is to make decisions based on the conventional rulings that govern every aspect of life. I would have expected him to look for answers only in the many books of law and interpretation that lined his shelves, and instead his story had emphasized the role of mature inner guidance in helping us find our way in uncharted waters. Studying and practicing Mussar help prepare us to make such choices by providing us with an honest awareness of ourselves and of life. Mussar steers us to take sure steps in life by giving us the tools with which to clear away whatever may be obstructing the guiding light of the soul. But it also tells us that it is only when we dive into the flowing waters of life itself that the soul will be given the cold-tempering that will make it as resilient and burnished as it can be.

I had been caught off guard by the rabbi's answer, which defied every prejudice I had ever held about the rigidity of hidebound Orthodoxy, but even more by the sudden surge of warmth I felt toward this man.

The time had come for me to leave, and in truth I was actually glad, because I needed some time to reflect upon and digest the many lessons I had learned that day. I thanked Rabbi Perr effusively for giving me so much of his time, for which I was truly amazed and appreciative. But his only response was to say, "My thanks must go to you."

I must have looked as baffled as that comment made me feel, because he went on, "You see, there is a danger in our practice, which is that it becomes a routine, it can become just a dry husk, just going through the motions. When I am with you, I see things through your eyes, it is so new, and it becomes fresh for me again."

Of course, I had hoped he would make me welcome, but I could not have anticipated the warm, respectful, and generous greeting I had received. I had spent six hours with him that day. The flank of his long black coat had been like a protective wing.

OPENING THE GATE

<small>MEDITATIONS TO DEVELOP
CONCENTRATION AND A CLEAR
AND FOCUSED MIND
AWARENESS 1</small>

The first and most essential quality Mussar calls upon us to develop is awareness. Clear and focused awareness is the foundation for the work we do to develop the traits of the soul. In the bright light of our own awareness, we are able to see with honesty who we are and the steps we need to take to become who we want to be. With awareness, we can see what life is about; without it, we stumble along in confusion.

Rabbi Perr introduced me to an awareness practice the first day we met. As he was driving me to the railroad station, I asked him if there was a Mussar practice I could take home with me to work on.

He thought a moment, then said, "Well, what you can do is get a rubber band that's big enough to fit around the palm of your hand. Keep it in your pocket, and when you feel impatient or angry, slip it on. No need to do anything more, just put it on." He looked over at me and smiled before turning back to the road.

I couldn't help feeling disappointed. In my readings I had come upon dramatic practices like repeating a stirring phrase "with lips aflame," or practicing awe-inspiring contemplations, so I had been hoping for something more profound than a rubber band. As I have used it, however, the rubber band has proved to be a remarkably effective little awareness tool. Just remembering to pull it out demands an act of awareness, and its gentle pressure on my skin also prods me to be present in the moment.

Later, when we discussed it, Rabbi Perr laughed as he told me that people sometimes asked him what color rubber band he recommended, or if he would give them *his* rubber band, as if its power would be enhanced by previous contact with the teacher.

Here's how it works for me. Imagine me sitting in my car waiting for my daughter after school. As every kid but her comes through the door, I become more and more impatient. Then I remember the rubber band. Just the act of remembering usually helps, because it makes me consciously aware of the impatience welling within me. As awareness kicks in, there appears in my mind's eye an identifiable group of sensations illuminated by the cool light of consciousness. The awareness prevents me from being swallowed up and carried away by those negative sensations, which might otherwise have led me to indulge in a full-blown temper tantrum.

Then, as I slip the rubber band over my hand, my aggrieved little soul is no longer alone in that car. I am suddenly joined by Rabbi Perr, all his students, the Mussar masters and great teachers of that tradition, and every other human being who ever fumed with impatience and struggled to master his emotion. What a party in the car! It's surprising there's any room left for my daughter when she finally opens the door to be greeted by my happy smile.

AWARENESS 2

*H*eshbon ha-Nefesh, a remarkable Mussar text written in the early nineteenth century by Rabbi Menachem Mendel Leffin, gives us another way to develop our awareness.

Rabbi Leffin tells the story of two young men who "took it upon themselves to pray with devotion, concentrating their attention on the meaning of the text." In the end, one of these men became misled in his prayer while the other became a famous scholar, a fine human being, and a great devotee of God.

"When asked how he had merited reaching this level, he replied: 'For many years I took it upon myself to focus my mind on a single thought—either Torah or prayer—for a specific period of time. By doing so, I eventually trained myself to be able to concentrate for an hour or even more.' "

What Rabbi Leffin describes here is a meditative form of prayer referred to in the Mussar tradition as *hitbonenut*, which translates to mean "to make oneself brilliantly aware." This kind of meditation develops the powers of concentration and a clear and focused mind.

In my youth, I learned to practice Buddhist meditation by focusing on and watching the in-and-out flow of my breath, and I still do that kind of meditation for twenty minutes or more every morning. But since I have been following a Jewish path, I have been spending time in prayer services on a regular basis, and I have found that meditating on a single word is a deepening, opening awareness practice I can also use.

I pick out and concentrate on one word from the service, allowing it to fill my entire mind. My effort is to illuminate that single word with consciousness. As other thoughts arise, I gently ease them aside, returning to the word. Sometimes the mind resists focus, offering up every rationalization to avoid the training. I can get lost in the train of my thoughts, one image carrying me to the next, but eventually I become aware of being lost, and that reminds me to return to the word.

The obvious words to concentrate on are the various names of God that occur in the liturgy, and sometimes I do that. But sometimes another word leaps out at me, and if it rings a bell, I go with it. For example, if I feel distracted, I might find myself drawn to the Hebrew word *shma,* which means "listen." I hold the sound and presence of the word on the screen of my consciousness, working gently to replace the movie that usually runs there with a single slide. The choice of word can be helpful, but the essence of the practice—no different from watching one's breath—is to still the mental chatter. Holding one's focus on a single word brings about concentration, which then gives rise to calmed space, clarity, and awareness.

Within such sharply present mental stillness, we catch glimpses of the dimension of our self that stands behind thought and identity and deeds. In Mussar, that dimension is named the soul.

CHAPTER TWO

THE GATE OF
THE SOUL

"The soul fills the body, as God fills the world. The soul bears the body, as God bears the world. The soul outlasts the body, as God outlasts the world. The soul is one in the body, as God is One in the world. The soul sees and is not seen, as God sees and is not seen. The soul is pure in the body, even as God is pure in the world . . ."

— RABBI SIMEON BEN PAZI,

THE TALMUD

After that first visit with Rabbi Perr, I had new inspiration to seek out and read Mussar texts, and I began a daily Mussar practice; but most importantly, Mussar began to infiltrate every aspect of my life, just as it is meant to do.

When I set out for Far Rockaway, my family apprehensively wondered if I would come back somehow radically different from the person who had gone. When I did return home, they were relieved to find that I was still recognizably me. I hadn't been converted to anything, and Mussar hadn't become my new religion. Still, as time went on, I know my wife noticed that the inner work I was doing was having an effect, because once, when Rabbi Perr called and she answered the phone, I overheard her thanking him for whatever contribution he had made toward giving her a husband who wasn't nearly as much of a pain as he'd been before. "I'm astonished," she told me he had responded. I never did clarify with him exactly what that meant. Was he amazed at how effective Mussar could be, or at the apparent fact that even such a hard nut as I was susceptible to cracking?

There is nothing in the world more precious to me than my family, so it astounds me now, looking back, to acknowledge how easy it was at times to take them all for granted—or, worse still, to behave toward them in ways that were nowhere near what I would have set for myself as ideal. When I was tired, I could be cranky. I could go months without complimenting Bev. If one of my daughters did something that didn't meet with my approval, I could become glacial and distant. I had such important things to do that I was often impatient with those who were closest to me. These aren't indictable offenses. They're just examples of the many ways in which I had allowed my life to drift along without even considering that I should be asking more of myself. As I slowly worked my way deeper into Mussar, however, I learned to be more aware of myself (there have been days when that rubber band got a lot of handling and stretching), and I was able to use that clearer vision to bring my attitudes and actions closer to my own ideals.

In Mussar, the most important practice we can do is to develop the intent to lift up our daily interactions, with others and with ourselves. Our relationships with other people are almost always where we face our biggest challenges, and so, if we look at them correctly, they can also be our richest opportunity to do the work on ourselves that will bring about profound and lasting inner changes.

But even as I and my family could see that these changes were slowly taking place in me, I was still troubled by doubts about whether it would be possible for me to follow a Mussar path and yet not become totally observant—what the Orthodox call *frum*. Mussar has never existed separately from Orthodoxy, and that first visit to the yeshiva and the world of Rabbi Perr had really brought home to me just how far from *frum* I was. These Orthodox people had had years of practice in their observances— from the smallest, like saying blessings before and after every meal, and after going to the bathroom, to the largest, such as respecting the rules of the Sabbath—and these rituals had long ago become part of their automatic and subconscious body-knowledge, while for me they were all sharply new and had to be performed with conscious intent. It was like everyone else was working with an electric food processor when all I had was a hand-grater and a knife. In the beginning there were plenty of nicks and scrapes.

I had felt no calling to become more observant. Mussar had come to me as a guiding light at a time when I had made a wasteland of my life, and I wanted more of that guidance. But black hats, the separation of men and women, mumbled prayers three times a day, a life of a million rules and regulations—I didn't see anything in Orthodoxy to draw me closer.

At that point I still didn't know whether I could have one without the other. Rabbi Perr hadn't really answered that question the first time I asked it, so on my second visit to Far Rockaway, about four months after the first, as we were sitting in his office following the daily *shmooze*, when for once the phone wasn't ringing and the workmen and students seemed to be engaged elsewhere, I took the opportunity to raise the issue again.

Before answering, he thought for a long moment, his fingers gently drumming on his pursed lips, which protruded from his beard. "Mussar was developed in the context of a *frum* world. It's hard to say where one begins and the other leaves off, but I'll try to answer you.

"First of all," he continued, leaning forward, as if that would help to get his point across, "it all revolves around the purpose. I have come to understand the observance of all the rules and the laws that we follow as the way to sanctify all of life. It's how we create a place for God's presence on earth. Mussar, on the other hand, is about bringing holiness into a *person*. That's the goal. For us, Mussar serves as part of the larger purpose, but it's almost an independent thing in its own right.

"Just because Mussar developed in a *frum* context," he asked rhetorically, "does that mean it has no significance outside of *frumkeit* [Orthodox observance]? That is absolutely not correct. For instance, if a gentile were to come to me for direction, I would teach him Mussar, but not *frumkeit*, because *frumkeit* doesn't apply to him."

"I've read that if a gentile wants to observe the Sabbath . . ." I started to interject, before he went on.

"He's not permitted," the rabbi finished for me. "But, nevertheless, I would be interested in teaching him kindness to other people and the extreme and clear understanding of what that implies, to the nth degree." That was his shorthand for Mussar. "It's like a car," he continued, giving me an analogy from a world I could more easily understand—much in the way he interpreted Mussar teachings for his students during his *shmoozes.* "You need all the parts to run the thing and to get where you're going, but many of the parts work on their own. The radio works as a radio, the water pump as a water pump. You don't need the whole car to play the radio. Of course, from my point of view, I've never seen anyone using a car radio anywhere but in a car. You know, with the car battery and its wiring and speakers all over the living room."

There was my answer. Mussar could be learned as a discipline without taking on the whole of the Orthodox culture that had birthed and sustained it, even though such a thing had never happened in Rabbi Perr's experience, or perhaps in anyone else's.

He let his eyes settle and remain on me. "I don't know if I've satisfied your question," he concluded, with a hopeful shrug.

To be sure that I had understood him correctly, I repeated back to him in my own words what I had heard. Elevating and purifying the inner life is an intrinsic spiritual value of the Orthodox world, I said, and Mussar had been developed within Orthodoxy to help people reach that goal. But someone who wasn't a part of that world might well share the Orthodox appreciation for refinement of the heart and soul, and in that case, the discoveries and disciplines of Mussar could be useful to that person, too.

When I had finished, he smiled and nodded his agreement. Perhaps there was some hope for this student after all.

Rabbi Perr then began to talk about what was really meant by refining the soul. "In the classical sources it says that a person is connected somehow to God," he said, "and that connection is the soul. The soul is not part of God, but it is a connection to God," he emphasized. "The soul is like the flame of a candle, the body being the wick."

Although we've all learned to think of ourselves as beings composed of body, mind, and spirit, Mussar tells us that these and all the other features of our lives—including the shadowy depths of the unconscious where our observing minds cannot probe—are intimately linked. They are all just faculties of the soul. That insight dissolves the resolute divorce of mind and body, inner and outer. You can no more separate them than you can detach a flame from the wick on which it burns.

Personally, I had never conceived of my inner reality in terms of "soul," and yet, in the earliest days of my Mussar exploration, I encountered teachings that insisted no one could take even a single step on the spiritual path without first coming to know the soul. At that point I had no idea what a soul was, or how I might begin to detect its presence within me, so I didn't really have a clue to where I should start if I wanted to get to know myself in terms of soul. And yet that was a threshold I just had to push through, because the teachings went on to say that whether we climb to the highest level of holiness, or stumble and fall to disgrace, it's all a matter of soul.

The Mussar tradition employs the three Hebrew words used in the Bible to refer to and describe various aspects of the soul, but even so, it cautions us not to think that the soul is made up of different anatomical parts. We have to understand clearly that naming three "parts" is only a device to help us discuss different aspects of the soul, which is difficult for us because, by its nature, the soul is not perceptible in the material world. But we can't let that deter us, since understanding the reality and the characteristics of the soul introduces us to the primary territory Mussar is meant to help us traverse.

Neshama is the most elevated and purest aspect of soul, and it shines at the deepest core of our being. "In my body he has kindled a lamp from his glory," begins a poem by Moses ibn Ezra, referring to the light of the *neshama*. At one point in a conversation with Rabbi Perr, when the topic of the *neshama* came up, he first quoted me a line from the morning prayers—"God, the soul [*neshama*] you have given me is pure"—and then he told me about a phone call he had received from a woman who was concerned about finding just the right school for her son, because she saw and loved his pure little *neshama*. "Parents want their children to be protected from the dangers in the world because they see such purity in those innocent *neshamas*," he said, a little smile on his lips, his head gently nodding.

The next dimension of the soul that Mussar identifies is called *ruach*, that aspect of the soul that is the source of animation and vigor—no more, and no less, than the "spirit of life."

Nefesh, the third level of the soul, is the aspect that is most visible and accessible to us. It includes all those inner aspects that link us to our lives on earth, including the physical body; so the body and soul are in fact a single, indivisible whole. Without the soul, the body is dust. Without sensation and the play of physical forces, the soul has no connection to the earth. It is the union of body and soul that gives rise to human experience.

The *nefesh* is the seat of all our emotions and appetites, the realm of personality and identity. If someone's *nefesh* is clear and unblemished, the light of the *neshama* will shine through without obstruction; if it is foggy, the light will be obstructed. Just as clouds determine how much sunshine makes it to earth, the *nefesh* acts as the "atmosphere" of our lives. The features of the soul that connect us to this world—personality, character, appetites, aversions, strengths, weaknesses—determine whether the holiness that is there at our core shines out or not, or to what degree. The goal of Mussar is to help us build up, or reduce, or balance the features of our life that cause the light within to brighten or dim, and so it focuses our attention on the *nefesh*.

The distinctive coloring and balance of the traits comprising the *nefesh* are what make each of us unique. Mussar offers us the valuable insight that each of us is actually endowed at birth with every single one of the full range of the human traits of character. The whole lot is seeded in us: anger is inborn, as are humility and love, worry and regret. And right from birth, each of us is inclined to a higher or lower measure of each of these traits. The things that draw you irresistibly send me fleeing. The quality in me that I just can't seem to stop tripping over is configured in you so that everyone loves and praises you for it.

What distinguishes one person from another is the *degree*, or *measure*, of the characteristics that live in each of our souls, and, while the Hebrew word for these traits—*middot*—is almost always translated as "traits of character," literally it does mean "measure." The angriest person, for example, has an excess of the anger trait, but Mussar insists that there is still some degree of calm within that raging soul. The stingiest person still possesses at least a grain of generosity, and even the most dishonest or lazy or arrogant individual will have some measure of the opposite within. It's not whether we have the traits—all of us have them all—but where we fall on the continuum that gives us our distinctive personality, our way of being in the world.

Then, as we age, and we are shaped by experiences and environment—or more deliberately by spiritual practices—every one of our thoughts and deeds comes to be inscribed in the soul. This causes the levels of our *middot* to be recalibrated. Sometimes excesses are reduced or deficiencies made up. Some tendencies will become ingrained as habits. We continue to be a home for every one of the soul-traits; only their levels change.

The practices that make up the Mussar discipline—meditation, contemplation, chanting, study, exercises, diary keeping, and the others that are given in the "Opening the Gate" sections of this book—have been developed and tested through the centuries, and have been found to be effective tools for the work of altering the levels of our soul-traits. A person is meant to assemble their own routine—traditionally under the guidance of a teacher—to custom-tune their daily discipline so it focuses on just those *middot* that are felt to need attention, whether because they are at too high a level, or too low, or because they cause ourselves or others suffering, or because we can just see that they are screening the holy light of the *neshama* from shining through.

When I delved into the Mussar texts, I found them full of guidance for understanding a variety of inner qualities—love and hate, pride and humility, mercy and cruelty, joy and worry, as well as many other familiar human traits—but in fact the lists given in these books aren't meant to tell us everything we need to know about the *middot*. They are provided simply as starting points for our own personal inner investigations.

If I'd been born into the Orthodox world and raised with soul awareness from birth, I might have had an intimate awareness of soul by the time I reached adulthood. But I wasn't, and so it was difficult for me to perceive that everything going on in my interior life was a function of soul. When I asked Rabbi Perr for guidance on how I could discover the reality of the soul within me, he acknowledged that this was not an easy thing to do directly. "You can't go about it scientifically," he said, "but I'm sure you've sometimes been touched deeply by poetry." His dark eyes turned inward for a moment, and I imagined him recalling some lines of verse that took him to that deep place. Then he added, "And the Vilna Gaon [the eminent eighteenth-century scholar to whom much of contemporary Orthodoxy can be traced] speaks of the profound impact of music on the soul. But," he concluded, "the most important thing you can do to know the soul is to observe yourself. It is because you are able to observe yourself that you can discover the soul, because it is the soul that is doing the observing."

With this encouragement to be introspective, and equipped with the map of the soul that Mussar provides, I set about developing a soul perspective. I gave myself the task of looking at every aspect of my inner life "as if" it were originating in the soul. So, for example, if I caught myself in the act of thinking, I would consciously note: "Thought is a faculty of the soul." Feelings, too, I would connect to the soul rather than viewing them as aspects of emotion. I would deliberately say to myself, "It is my soul that is joyful," or "My soul is filled with sadness." I even included my body in this practice, so that, as my hand was reaching for something, I'd comment that it was soul that was reaching out.

Over time, this exercise came to have a lasting effect. Gradually the hypothesis—acting "as if" I had a soul—actually started to ring true. At first there were just brief moments when I did perceive the soul. Then, as the insight took hold, instead of being just a mental exercise it became an increasingly comfortable reality. I went from looking at myself as if I had a soul to actually experiencing my life *as* a soul.

For me, one of the most enlightening aspects of this new way of seeing had to do with the way I came to view the very process of thought. If you'd asked me before I began my Mussar practice, I would have told you that thought originates in the mind, the same way I'd tell you that bile originates in the gall bladder, because we've all been conditioned to think of the mind as a physical organ, comparable to the liver and kidneys. But in fact, while the brain is certainly an organ, the mind is not so tangible. It may be just a convenient way for us to label and segregate the mental processes. The more I learned of Mussar, the more I came to realize that there was no real reason to separate these processes at all. We know in our lives that ideas can affect the emotions just as feelings can impact the body, so seeing all of these aspects of ourselves as functions of the soul restores the unity that they actually seem to have.

With this understanding, which Mussar urges us not only to "know" but to integrate into ourselves so deeply that it becomes a feature of our "awareness," we come to see that our mental functions are simply one of the many faculties of the soul, along with memory, emotion, the unconscious, and all the other aspects of who we are. These are all aspects of the undivided inner being.

A soul perspective knits the inner life back into a whole, without for a second denying the reality and distinctiveness of thought, feeling, the physical body, and all the other attributes we know in our lives. And it makes a place for those human traits that don't fit comfortably into the tripartite scheme of mind/body/spirit. Take wisdom for example. Where does it reside? In the mind? The body? The emotions? Only when we see it as a faculty of the soul does wisdom fit comfortably into the map of our inner being, alongside all our other faculties.

As these insights took hold, I came to see the soul as a precious gift I wanted to care for with love. I began to feel compelled to cut through whatever blockages were obstructing my way to realizing the fullest potential of the soul, which is revealed when we uncover and live in the light of holiness that shines within. And as I took little steps and made a little progress in that direction, these ideas infiltrated my behavior. It wouldn't really matter if I had perceived that my actions emanate from the soul unless that perception changed the way I acted. I began to find myself asking whether what I was about to do was good for my soul, and that was a new influence on the choices I made. When I looked into the eyes of the person across from me, was that a soul I saw? When I did see a soul, in myself or in another, kindness and consideration seemed to arise naturally.

The result was that my old resistance to things that were "good for me"—like exercise, and better nutrition, and getting more sleep—began to erode. And my relationships with other people began to be enlivened with more warmth and caring.

OPENING THE GATE

LEARNING HOW TO READ A
SPIRITUAL TEXT

I learned a lot about the soul from Rabbi Perr, but I learned as well from the small clutch of Mussar books that have been written over the last ten centuries. The teachers in the tradition have made a priority of putting together a map of the soul that is revealed in depth and detail in Mussar classics like *The Duties of the Heart, The Palm Tree of Deborah,* and *The Path of the Just.* Reading and absorbing the insights of texts like these has always been and remains a central activity in the practice of Mussar.

It was through reading that I was first challenged to see that my life is actually the life of a soul, and reading also gave me an array of key concepts that I now use to understand what I am finding as I go. The Mussar classics provide a framework to help us make sense of where we are in the world, and also of the path of transformation that lies before us.

But I had to learn how to read a Mussar text. It wasn't just that these books are mostly centuries old, and are written in language and with cultural biases that we stumble over today. There is also a traditional way that these books are meant to be not just read, but studied. Ideally the journey of learning from them is shared with a teacher or a partner. You don't just read through, chapter by chapter, as you would a novel. Instead, you dip in for just a few lines at a time. You read them, then you step back and compare what you find in the book to your own experience. You examine and discuss your own life in relation to the teaching, looking for ways in which you are or aren't fulfilling the ideas you've understood. You may want to take notes. This way, you not only absorb the substance of the teaching but also gain insight into yourself.

Through the self-examination that accompanies study you may discover that there is a gap between how you are living your life and what is written in the book. In that case, you need to study that same section again and again, going over it until it becomes perfectly clear and makes a deep impression. This awakens you to what is written in the book and causes its lesson to penetrate deeply. In addition, reading can reveal where you need to do inner work, and can also provide guidance on Mussar practices that might help you in just those areas that have been uncovered.

As an example, there is a small chapter in the eleventh-century text *The Duties of the Heart*, by Bahya ibn Pakuda, that I now use in my teaching. The title is "How to Be Moved to Repentance." The answer the author gives is that there are four main motivators, which he lists in order of priority. He says that the best way to be prodded to elevate our inner traits is "by acutely realizing God's presence . . ." He carries on from there, but as readers we need to stop right at this point.

Do we understand what he means by "acutely realizing God's presence"? We can see that there are actually two different ideas here: acute realization *and* God's presence. To get the benefit of this teaching, we need to make space in which to consider for ourselves—and also to look for answers elsewhere, in this and other books—how we might go about giving ourselves this acute realization—and where we can look for God's presence. The answers are there. But we won't find them if we just race right over that one opening phrase. We're not meant to read through lightly, but to study and learn, precious bit by precious bit.

It can take a long time to read a Mussar book that way. It is said that Rabbi Israel Salanter took nine years to read his way through *The Path of the Just*. But is there any better way to spend our time, if we are absorbing ideas that help us to reflect and to learn and, most important, to grow?

CHAPTER THREE

THE GATE OF
GROWING

"And you shall circumcise the foreskin of your heart."

— DEUTERONOMY 10:16

*"And the Eternal One, your God, will circumcise your
heart and the heart of your seed."*

— DEUTERONOMY 30:6

I
t took time for the soul perspective to take root as the natural way for me to look upon all aspects of my inner and
outer life, but once it had become firmly established, I
found that I wanted to do whatever I could to nurture and take
care of my soul—which meant, in effect, to nurture and take
care of my life.

Our efforts to improve or heal those traits of character that
are obscuring the light of our soul is how we elevate ourselves,
and reveal the radiance of holiness that lives within. This desire
to rise up, heal, and improve is innate in all human beings, I believe. Of course, we all slip and tumble too, but the drive to get
up and push on that lives deep in all of us is what compels us to

keep trying. Some of us set out to do great and difficult things, like saving the rain forests or finding a cure for cancer, but it would be a rare and pathological individual, I think, who didn't agree that it's worth some effort even just to bring more love and caring and satisfaction into his or her own life.

Rabbi Perr and I were sitting and talking in the living room of his house one day when I mentioned this hypothesis to him, and he not only knew exactly what I meant, but added that he thought it was the same innate human drive that causes us to do the simple everyday things, like shining our shoes and bringing more kindness to our relationships.

In Mussar, this improvement is called *tikkun ha-middot:* improving or healing the traits of character. Because Mussar tells us that everything we do in our daily lives presents an opportunity for this kind of self-improvement, Rabbi Perr sees even a simple chore like sewing on a button or mending a hole in his sock as "doing a *tikkun.*"

"People take apart and repair things and have a great *nachas* [satisfaction] from that," he said. "I myself have a great *nachas* from repairing a broken alarm clock. Nobody appreciates it. People say, 'Throw it out, it's a piece of junk.' But I hate throwing it out. I take the thing apart, I repair it, and I put it together again. I'm very happy with it, but who do I show it off to? My students have no interest, my wife has no interest, my kids think I'm nuts. But I have *joy* doing it. Why? Because it gives me a wonderful sense of doing a *tikkun.* We all have that; it's innate."

That seemed right—I think we all do have a deeply felt urge to make things better—and I told him I thought that was a wonderful thing.

"Yes," he agreed, "a tremendous thing. But you have to develop that sense, you've got to develop a taste for doing that."

I would be the last to disagree. Developing that "taste" has become an ongoing process for me, the focus of my Mussar practice; but how, I wondered aloud, did others, particularly the great Mussar teachers, develop and perfect it?

My question gave Rabbi Perr another opportunity to talk about one of his favorite subjects—his late father-in-law, Rabbi Yehudah Leib Nekritz. "Novarodock was his tradition, of course," Perr reminded me. Of the three branches that emerged within the Mussar movement, Novarodock followed the most radical discipline for change. Its founder, Rabbi Yosef Yozel Hurvitz, began his spiritual career by having himself bricked into a small room for two years of intense self-inquiry. Later in life, he retreated to a forest hut for nine years. "Mussar at Novarodock," Rabbi Perr continued, "was not just to take off a person's flaws, it was really a way of life, a way of growth, and my father-in-law knew that. Mussar gave him life. He used to say that he was one hundred percent the product of Mussar."

He paused, nodded, then added, "You know, he used to say about himself, 'People say that before Mussar, Yehudah Leib was smooth as silk. And after Mussar . . .' And he would never complete that sentence. What I think is that he never finished the sentence because, to his mind, the qualities he had acquired from Mussar practice were sublime. They made silk appear as coarse raw material, and he had no words to describe them."

And how, I asked, might the rest of us approach that kind of growth?

Rabbi Perr plucked at his beard. "That's an interesting question," he said. Then, reflectively, he added, "A very good question. There's been a great debate about that—the question of where the most powerful growth is going to come from. Is it from studying the Torah or studying Mussar, and how much effort should be devoted to each?

"When Rabbi Israel Salanter was faced with this question, he said that Torah is a *segulah* [a charm] and Mussar is like *refuah* [medicine]. The difference is that a charm works without our understanding how." He leaned back then, resting his elbows on the arms of his chair, looking at me over the tops of his glasses, preparing to tell a story. "Like a guy might have an amulet from a saintly person, and he's sick, and he puts it on in the proper way, says the proper verses of Psalms, and becomes well. He doesn't know why it worked, he doesn't know how, he just knows that it worked. But if the amulet is written improperly, or if he put it on wrong, it wouldn't work.

"Medicine," he continued, "doesn't work that way. Medicine is rational. Medicine works because, by trial and error, certain discoveries have been made. So what Rabbi Salanter was saying is that Torah can cure a person, but it works like an amulet. The Torah has to be studied in a certain way, for the sake of heaven, with purity and devotion. If those characteristics are lacking—if it's studied in the wrong way—it won't take care of your problems. But Mussar is like medicine. You have a headache, you take an aspirin, it works!"

Mrs. Perr had come into the room while her husband was telling this tale. She took a seat and listened quietly. Mrs. Perr's father had insisted that his daughter be well educated, and she now works as a social worker, both in private practice and in Jewish girls' schools. He also had seen to it that she was educated in Mussar, and so, when Rabbi Perr took a breath, she offered a teaching of her own. "A young man," she said, "once came to ask Rabbi Salanter whether he should learn Mussar or Torah, since he had only one hour a day for study." The question concealed a challenge, because it was asking the rabbi to state outright whether he supported the priority traditionally granted to Torah study in Jewish practice, or whether he thought Mussar should be ranked first. Mrs. Perr smiled as she told me his answer: " 'Study Mussar,' he said. 'Then you'll discover that you have more than one hour in the day to study.' "

Rabbi Perr then added, "That's a marvelous story, because it means that if you do Mussar, you are going to reorder the priorities in your life."

That was it, then. Following the Mussar discipline causes far-reaching change. I had come across a phrase at different places in the Bible that gives an image of just how this process of change is meant to happen, and while I had an intuitive sense that there was wisdom in it that related to my own journey of discovery, I didn't really understand what it meant. So I took the opportunity to ask Rabbi Perr what he understood to be the meaning of "circumcise the foreskin of your heart."

He answered almost immediately. "It says circumcise the heart because we are so closed." He shook his head and repeated, more softly, sadly, "We are so closed.

"People say 'I can't believe this is happening.' Why? Because we can't absorb the experience. Why can't we absorb the experience? That's because of *orlas ha-lev,* the foreskin of the heart.

'Callousness,' we'd call it today—not allowing feelings to pene-trate, not allowing oneself to be soft, to have pity."

Then he defined what he meant by "heart," a word that is central to all Mussar teachings. "The *lev* [heart]," he said, "rep-resents the deeper feelings where the intellect and emotions blend."

The intellect and emotions are not to be thought of as sepa-rate. There is a place where they live together, and that is in the heart, at our very center.

A recent Mussar master has described this calloused condi-tion as *timtum ha-lev*. *Timtum* means "stopped up," and in this context describes a spiritual insensitivity resulting from the blocked flow of our inner life.

But what is the source of this blockage? With every betrayal, slight, conflict, abuse, or loss, the heart can become a bit more hardened and closed as, layer upon layer, the anger and hatred build up to wall off our inner core. This is how the ego attempts to protect us from the barbs of life, but ultimately it is a strategy that must fail, because people who never succeed in opening their hearts leave their sweetest self imprisoned behind that wall. But it's never too late to experience a "circumcision" of the heart.

"Yes," Rabbi Perr added, "the penetration of the heart is what we're seeking."

The biblical story of Jonah gives us a model of the journey to an open heart. Jonah is onboard a ship, trying to avoid the des-tiny God has planned for him. A great storm develops and will only abate when Jonah is thrown overboard to begin the darkest leg of his journey.

The Bible tells us clearly that the crew on Jonah's ship didn't want to throw him overboard, which means that it was Jonah himself who brought about the descent that was the start of his transformative passage.

The story is telling us that the journey of transformation begins with our taking action. We must not be afraid to dive down into the depths. We must not be passive, for it is only we ourselves who can initiate the process of our own spiritual renewal.

As Jonah descends to the very depths of the sea, the description of his slide makes it explicit that he is diving into the depths of his soul: "The waters surrounded me. Even to the soul," it reads.

When he has reached the darkest depths, Jonah cries out to God. He has penetrated to the inner reaches of his soul, and his heart is opened. That is the meaning of his cry. And what is the result? "You brought up my life from the pit," Jonah says to God, and at that moment, he begins his spiritual ascent.

Calling this transition a circumcision lets us know that it is a kind of initiation, and that, like an actual circumcision, it can be a difficult experience. When the protective shell that we allow to grow up over our heart is cut or broken or smashed, it exposes the tenderness beneath, and that can be painful.

Sometimes, in their wisdom, people make the choice to open their hearts and lead themselves to their own spiritual initiation. Sometimes life itself delivers the severing blow. For me, it was a combination of the two. Ambition and pride had laid layer upon layer of callus over my heart, until the collapse of my business came as a cleaving blow that sliced right through that shell and exposed my vibrant core once again. At the beginning it was painful, but those feelings were a message that I had been restored to life, and as my breath and the fuller range of feelings came back to me, I made the conscious choice to learn and to change in ways that would prevent those layers from ever growing back. The Mussar curriculum is dedicated to cleansing the heart, and I willingly took to it in the hope that it would help me keep my heart from ever stopping up again.

I saw something like this happen to my mother, too. In her early eighties, she went through my father's protracted illness and death, and right behind that the deaths of her two sisters. More alone than she had ever been, and confronted with the hard realities of her own aging, she grieved deeply, but when she had done enough of that, she made a decision not to go the route of shriveling and hardening that curses many people's last years. "If I'm going to be alive," she seemed to say to herself, "then I think I should be just as alive as I can be."

For the next—and last—five years of her life, there could have been no more active, engaged, lively person. It didn't matter whether I called her morning, noon, or night, her answering machine became my closest friend. If she wasn't playing cards with her buddies, she was doing a round of visiting in the hospital, or attending a lecture. When we cleaned out her apartment after she died, we found bags of wool and half a dozen newly knitted pairs of slippers that she had made to give away to friends. There were three freshly baked cakes in the fridge and several tins of home-baked cookies she had prepared for parties she was planning to attend. There were two bags of potato latkes: one for friends and one for the family Chanukah party she was looking forward to. This was the kitchen productivity of a nearly ninety-one-year-old woman! When my sisters were with her in her last hours in the hospital, calls kept coming from someone with an unfamiliar name. Finally they took the call, and it turned out to be Mom's buddy from the grade-five class at the local school, who had become dismayed when Mom did not attend a class Chanukah party that day.

The combined power of loss, aging, and mortality cut through the *orlah* of her heart. It was a very painful time, but it taught her a great lesson, one that she passed on to us: life is about growing. When something didn't work in her life, she tried to fix it. When something did work, she tried to stretch to a further goal. She's a model for me as I reach out to know and penetrate the layers of my own inner being—to grow.

Early on, it was pain that kept my heart awake, and it seemed impossible that my heart would ever settle back into the state of hardened dullness from which it had been wrenched. My heart beat loudly in my life, and I remember my sister responding uncomfortably to the unusually loving e-mails I sent her at that time. But as the storm in my life subsided and the pain abated, I began to feel the pull of gravity dragging my center back into its old and habitual ruts. It would take conscious effort to counter that force, and to keep my heart at the forefront of my concerns. I learned then why Mussar was meant to be a daily discipline. By resolutely keeping at the learning and practice, it eventually became ingrained in my thinking that every thought, word, and act has some effect in either opening or closing the heart. And by remembering to treasure my open heart, I developed the inclination to weigh my choices and try always to make the ones that had me reaching toward opening, always opening.

As I pursued this way of living, either I'd feel the satisfaction of having made a choice that brought more vitality to my heart, or I'd feel that I'd just received a lesson in living. One way or the other, I knew Mussar was helping me to bring more vibrancy to my life.

There's another term used frequently in Mussar that also refers to the process of "opening up," but in a different context. It's the Yiddish word *derherin*. *Her* means to hear, and *derher* means that you hear something in a way that makes a difference, that you don't just hear it but allow it to *penetrate*.

Rabbi Perr told me a story about this way of hearing that made us both laugh, even as it clearly explained what it means to hear in this way.

"There was once a person," he said, "who had never seen the railroad. So he went down to see it, and what he saw were the tracks. He thought that was the whole railroad, so he sat down and started to examine the rails. Then there was a 'toot toot,' and the people who were standing near him said, 'The horn! The horn!' 'I hear, I hear,' he replied. 'Isn't it wonderful?' 'No,' the people said, 'the whistle . . .' but he just continued to sit there because he heard the whistle and he thought it was a wonderful thing. Finally, the people were so frightened they didn't know what to do, and someone cried out, 'You have to *derher*, not just *her!*' " Rabbi Perr spluttered with laughter at that one. "It's not enough just to hear the horn, you have to understand that a train is coming. *Gevalt!*" And now he laughed long and deep.

To *derher* is to listen with your whole being, not just with your ear or your mind. When the fortified layers of the heart are pierced, the core of your being is exposed and made receptive so that you can hear life's messages deeply and directly, with the wisdom of the soul.

Mussar tells us that it is up to us to open our hearts so that we can hear the penetrating truths, not just the sounds that come into our ears. But how do we do that? I tried to get Rabbi Perr to give me some practical tips to take home with me. I was pushing him at that point, and he knew it.

"You know," he said gently, "what's important is to be on the trip, not to get there. The importance is to study the book, not to finish it. Particularly for people of our age, who are set in their habits, the way to do something is, first of all, to work at it slowly and gradually. As we mellow, so do our flaws and our weaknesses mellow, until they are much reduced.

"I want to tell you—and I think this is very important—that if our children or ourselves come back from school with an eighty-five or ninety, we should be happy even though it's not a hundred. There's no reason why we should demand perfection of ourselves or others. We don't all have to get one hundreds. If we get an eighty-five or ninety, and we've come up from a sixty-five or seventy, we should be very pleased. We destroy ourselves looking for the hundred when we don't look for a hundred in anything else."

That was a good thing for me to hear, because I tend to get down on myself when I focus only on the steps I haven't taken rather than on the ones I've already covered. He was also cautioning me not to fall into one of the biggest potholes on the Mussar path. Because Mussar focuses on healing our flaws and our weaknesses, there is a real danger that we will focus only on the negative and whip ourselves over those traits that aren't yet cooked to perfection. Some Mussar teachers have done just that, and have been very shrill in their demand for self-reproach. But while this might work for some people, it doesn't for me. It doesn't give me spiritual energy.

"It's important to look at the steps you have taken," Rabbi Perr said, smiling softly. "The Alter of Novarodock said that when you walk, if you look at the place where you want to go, it seems to be very far away. But if you look down at how your feet are walking, they seem to be traveling very rapidly."

Our jet-age, results-oriented way of thinking runs counter to the slow, gradualist approach of the European Mussar way. "People," said the Alter of Novarodock, "want to achieve greatness overnight, and to sleep well that night too." Rabbi Perr believes that true and lasting change can happen only at the deepest levels of the soul, and comes very slowly. Rabbi Israel Salanter likened the Mussar practice to "drops of water which, if they fall drop by drop over the stone for many days and years, will wear it away, even though the first drop was not even felt . . ."

Rabbi Perr knew what he wanted to tell me at the end of that day. "The trip," he said, "takes a long time to complete, if ever. The most important thing is to be on the boat, or the plane, or whichever vehicle you're on." His voice lifted then. "It's a mirage to think there is an end." Then it dropped. "I don't know if there is an end." He paused a few seconds, eyes down, stroking his beard. Then he looked up. "And why should one seek an end?

"You know, you meet stunted people who have stopped growing along the way. You meet them every day. It's just a wonderful thing to continue to grow."

OPENING THE GATE

Rabbi Israel Salanter built the Mussar movement to provide people with practices that would foster inner growth. It is said that one night, as he walked past the home of a shoemaker, Rabbi Salanter noticed that despite the late hour, the man was still working by the light of a dying candle. "Why are you still working?" he asked. "It is very late and soon that candle will go out." The shoemaker replied, "As long as the candle is still burning, it is still possible to accomplish and to mend." This image so captured Salanter's imagination that he spent that entire night excitedly pacing his room and repeating to himself: "As long as the candle is still burning, it is still possible to accomplish and to mend."

With just that possibility in mind, Rabbi Salanter innovated a practice that is well documented in the lore of the Mussar movement. He encouraged his students to recite phrases that in some way related to the particular character trait they were working on at the time. He even founded a string of "Mussar houses" where students could go to study and to practice in this way, strengthened by the company of others.

A person trying to rein in his tendency to gossip, for example, might choose the traditional phrase, "Do not go as a tale-bearer among your people." For shyness, there is "You shall not fear the face of any man." The phrase doesn't have to be biblical; it can come from any wisdom source, as long as it conveys the essence of the trait the individual is trying to enhance or diminish.

The basic practice is to repeat this phrase over and over, for as long as it takes to shake it loose of the intellect so that it can carry its message directly to the heart. But simply saying the phrase is not enough. Rabbi Salanter insisted that the repetition be done aloud, with great emotion. It is essential that it be chanted "with lips aflame," to use his own words, and the name he gave this practice was *hitpa'alut*, meaning "with intense emotional excitement."

He saw that this practice had great transformative effect. Because the desires that drive us to sin and suffering are propelled by emotion and arise from the unconscious, he believed that the antidote also had to be emotional and reach equally deeply into the depths of the unconscious. He recognized that the emotions can act as levers to pry open the heart, and he had the insight to understand that lessons implanted in this way would take root at the most profound inner level, where the light of the intellect never shines. Although the intellect and learning play important roles in Mussar's transformative process, what we learn by way of the intellect simply doesn't have the capacity to uproot and refigure inner traits so directly.

Personally, I've had good success with this practice. I used it to help me with a problem that afflicted me when I got myself all tied up in fear of embarrassing myself by saying or doing something wrong at the yeshiva in the midst of ritual and prayer. It was obvious to me that I was too concerned with what others might think of me, a common enough ailment, and I wanted to bring myself back to a deeper and more wholesome motivation for thought and action.

I was worried about loss of honor, and I understood that this was the voice of my ego speaking. I didn't want to cater to the ego's claims, but neither did I want to still its self-aggrandizing voice as if self-abasement were the greater virtue. No particular trait, including honor, is intrinsically good or bad; the goal is to find balance, and to use the trait in a positive way.

For my practice, I chose the biblical phrase from Leviticus that says, "You shall be holy." This worked for me because it took my attention entirely away from the ego and caused me to focus on the elevation of the soul.

I recited my phrase in a quiet room by myself. I began slowly and quietly. The effect of speaking the words aloud was very surprising. Immediately, I was addressing myself directly and deeply. As I continued, I began to pick up the volume and the intensity of feeling I gave to the words. The emotion I brought to the recitation could best be described as exaltation. I let the emphasis fall on different words: *You* shall be holy. You *Shall* be holy. You shall be *Holy*. And each new emphasis said something different to me.

It turned out that I didn't need to do this for very long, because my phrase soon took root and grew inside me. As I pushed through the doors of the study hall for prayers, the queasy fear of humiliation met the phrase there in my mind. "You shall be holy." That set my priorities straight. Could I still be holy if my *tefillin* strap got twisted or even slipped down my arm? With that thought in mind, I was able to laugh at myself as I smiled and nodded to those around me, and went to take my place in the hall.

CHAPTER FOUR

THE GATE OF HOLINESS

"Holiness is twofold. Its beginning is labor and its end reward; its beginning exertion and its end, a gift."

—RABBI MOSHE CHAIM LUZZATO,

THE PATH OF THE JUST

In the biblical text, when Jacob awakens after his dream of the ladder, he says, "How awesome is this place. It must be God's temple. It is the gate to heaven." The climb up Jacob's ladder takes us to a holy place, and what we find for ourselves at the top is holiness. I knew, of course, both from my own studies and from previous discussions with Rabbi Perr, that I might never reach that ultimate rung of the ladder, but that didn't trouble me nearly as much as the realization that I didn't really have an inkling of what such a state of being might feel like or even what holiness might be.

I'd first come across a reference to holiness as the goal of Mussar practice in the classic source *The Path of the Just*, written by Rabbi Moshe Chaim Luzzatto in the eighteenth century. Luzzatto doesn't actually say much about holiness until the very last chapter, and there he describes those who have reached this sanctified level: "The holy, those who constantly attach themselves to God, and whose souls move about in the true notions of love and reverence for the Creator, are considered to be walking before God in the land of the living while they are in this world. The very person of this sort of human being is considered to be a tabernacle, sanctuary, and altar." He says that when a person is graced with holiness, "a spirit from on high will descend upon you, and the Creator will dwell on you as He does all of His holy ones."

Those are daunting words. Luzzatto makes holiness seem so otherworldly and beyond anything in my own earthbound experience. He also never really tells us what holiness is. But he is so emphatic that holiness is the ultimate goal to which Mussar practice leads that I knew I had to come to some understanding of what it means. That led me back to Rabbi Perr.

I found him in his office, and when he saw me his eyes smiled. I'd often noticed the warmth and pleasure with which he greeted people, even though, each time, the happiness he radiated seemed fresh and new. That day, his hat sat on his desk, and on his head he wore instead a black *yarmulke*. Without the volume of his tall round hat to balance it, his long square beard seemed fuller than ever. He invited me to sit, and, with traffic noises, thuds, and the occasional shout from a workman playing in the background like some kind of discordant soundtrack, I asked my question, referring to that enigmatic description in the last chapter of Luzzatto's book.

"You know," he began, "when I teach that book, I always teach the last chapter first. Why? Well, the main reason doesn't actually have anything to do with holiness. But in that chapter Luzzatto explains that his book needs to be used relative to one's own life. The path for one person is not the same as the path for another. I think it's important for a seeker to hear that when starting out, so he understands that he's not supposed to follow the book and the discipline like a straitjacket. That's why I teach it first."

Right there, Rabbi Perr had touched exactly upon one of the reasons I was so drawn to Mussar: it doesn't propose a one-size-fits-all spiritual path. It has always seemed to me that when people, in all their diversity, get crammed into any preordained conceptual framework, all the odd angles and sharp edges that make each of us so wonderfully unique get sheared off, like cheese forced into a mold, and what's left is somehow less than a whole. Mussar, on the other hand, teaches that, because each of us will naturally find different soul-traits presenting themselves as challenges in our lives, we each have our own qualities to cultivate; and, as we ascend toward the place where our soul will blossom, the holiness that emerges in each of us has its own time, shape, and colors. As we move toward this state of completion, we don't all start to look uniform, with the same identical traits, but rather grow into a richer, more balanced, more beautiful version of who we already are.

There is a story told about Zusya, a Chassidic teacher who was dying, and he was weeping.

"Why are you crying, Rebbe?" his disciples asked.

"I'm crying because after I die, I am going to face my day of judgment," he sobbed.

"But Rebbe," his students protested, "you've lived such a pure life! You couldn't have been more like Moses himself!"

"Don't you see?" Reb Zusya responded. "When I stand before that heavenly court, they're not going to ask me why I wasn't more like Moses! They're going to ask me why wasn't I more like Zusya!"

That's Mussar's purpose: help us become the fullest version of the unique soul we already are.

Rabbi Perr shifted in his chair, adjusted his coattails, and then got back to the question I had originally asked.

"I can't tell you what holiness is exactly," he said. "In Hebrew, the word *kadosh*, which we translate as 'holiness,' has a sense of otherness, of separation, like the separation of a pure essence, without contamination or impurity. But I can tell you that I've had the privilege of seeing holy people. I've seen people who have purified my eyes just by looking at them. In some faces, it's as if I can see the Divine Image in which they were created.

"I know, I know," he added quickly, holding up his hands as if to fend me off. "God says not to picture Him. But still, instinctually we do form some kind of image, and for me it's what I've seen in a holy face."

He smiled softly, raising his caterpillar eyebrows, and then he said, "Maybe you'll see it one day too. When you do, you'll know about holiness just from the experience."

Then, dark eyes sparkling, he added, "Maybe you'll even see it in the mirror one day."

We both laughed, and I laughed harder. It felt so ridiculous for me even to think of myself in those terms. I confess, though, that I feel sometimes in my quietest moments, in meditation and in prayer, the deep longing to bring greater spirit to my life. And I'm inspired to seek the holy here, now, within me, not because I must or because I fear punishment in the afterlife, but because

I can. Luzzatto tells us that through our spiritual practice we can come to a state of inner wholeness—what he calls *shlemut*—right here on earth.

When I remarked to Rabbi Perr that in English the relationship between wholeness and holiness is evident simply in the words themselves, he shared with me his own ideas about *shlemut* (or, as he says it in the pronunciation of the yeshiva world, "*shlemus*").

"I think," he began, "that it would be a disservice to say that the original meaning of *shlemus* was anything other than 'perfection.' The point was not to compromise, because if there is even a tiny flaw remaining, it's going to fester and come back. It's like a doctor wanting to get every cell when he's removing a cancer. You want to remove every cell of every flaw in yourself. But that creates a standard it's very hard for us to live by today."

He paused then, and it seemed to me that he was trying to decide how deeply he ought to go into this subject; but it is so central to Mussar that, after a moment, he continued.

"It's also possible to say that instead of 'perfection without a flaw,' *shlemus* might mean 'roundedness' or 'wholeness.' There will certainly be those who debate me on this, but I base myself on something I once heard from my wife's grandfather, my teacher Rabbi Avraham Yoffen, who explained the saying of the sages that states, 'A person is required to say: "When will my actions come to the level of Abraham, Isaac, and Jacob?" ' So, the question is asked, who can come to the level of these heroes of the past, the founders of our people? There is a lot of discussion about what that means, and Rabbi Yoffen explained that of course you can't *be* Abraham, Isaac, and Jacob. But there is such a thing as a very large picture of part of a face. You could have a billboard twenty feet high and forty feet across showing only a part of a face. Or you can have a small picture of a whole face. Rabbi Yoffen used to say that the sages meant that we should be a picture of a whole face, and in that way we would be like Abraham, Isaac, and Jacob. Of course, we're not going to be the big billboard that they were, but just because we can't be the big billboard doesn't mean we have to be only part of a face. Be whole! And that opens the door to understanding *shlemus* not as perfection but as wholeness."

That seemed to me a useful way of interpreting the concept, but for Rabbi Perr the debate wasn't over. The distinction between perfection and wholeness is not trivial, and he knew it. Searching for perfection directs us toward a sacred way of being that takes us to the pinnacle of this world and even beyond, but we can seek wholeness without detaching from the brokenness and imperfection littered all around us. He leaned back, set his elbows on the arms of his chair, clasped his hands together, and settled in for the next round. The tradition of interpreting Torah that he follows invites him to take his ideas into new territory, but only so long as he does not break completely from the ideas that are inherited. He needed to justify his thoughts in those terms.

"Defining *shlemus* as 'wholeness' also has problems," he went on. "It has problems because it's modern, and there's no proof of it, even though it makes a lot of sense. But it has another problem as well, which is that without focusing, without specializing, it's very hard to get anywhere. People who try to go in many directions at the same time don't travel anywhere. So the danger is that if you say 'wholeness' instead of 'perfection,' you may not get anywhere. You could get scattered. To get somewhere you have to stay focused.

"I'm very, very concerned about not misleading others. That's a fundamental concern of mine. So, promulgating a judgment or opinion of roundedness rather than perfection is a dangerous thing to do, and I constantly seek out sources to support my view. But still, I think it has a certain legitimacy. Perhaps it's a little easier for us to think of *shlemus* as wholeness rather than perfection, but I don't need to excuse myself for making excuses for us because I really do believe we're a weaker generation. We're a more distracted generation. I've had the privilege of studying with some really great people, and I see the difference."

"Would you say those people were perfected?" I ventured.

"Closer than I," he said softly, "closer than I. And I'm not saying that out of humility. The ones before me . . . there is just no comparison. When you met them, you knew there was a God. There was no question that . . . that this was not an ape." And then he repeated, almost in a whisper, "Not an ape with clothes on."

We shared a good laugh. He made the notion that there was more animal than angel in such holy people seem as silly as saying the moon was made of cheese.

Having completed his debate with the invisible adversaries of tradition, Rabbi Perr brought the conversation back to the place where Mussar always, ultimately, focuses, which is in the here-and-now.

"Seeking a very high goal lifts you," he said. "Talking about perfection lifts you. The challenge is to change and become the person you would like to be: mellow, unafraid, wise . . . to be like people I have seen, never in a rush, never lost, never confused, always with the right answers, facing life with equanimity, for themselves and for others—that's what I feel is the ultimate goal, what I would love to be. And I see Mussar as a very good vehicle for achieving that, both in its exercises and in its views. Mussar is the practical discipline for becoming holy.

"What a person can do," he went on, "is to put himself on the path by sanctifying his deeds."

I knew what he meant by that because the notion of sanctifying one's deeds also comes from *The Path of the Just*. Whether or not we attain holiness, Luzzatto tells us, depends on our own behavior. First, we must separate ourselves from anything that exerts a negative influence on our soul. After that, we must sanctify our deeds, which means to act positively by bringing a spirit of consecration to every one of our actions, no matter how secular and mundane.

Once the idea of sanctifying deeds had sunk roots into my mind, it began to show up unbidden throughout my life. Just as I'd be lifting a fork to my mouth, the idea of consecrating the act would pop into my head. I'd stop for a second to look at the food in front of me, and I'd realize what a miracle it is that sunlight is converted into food that nourishes and sustains my body. But then I'd be suddenly aware, too, of just how complex is the simple act of eating, and I could no longer just chomp away unconsciously without a thought for the earth and the rain that generate the harvest. That thought then led me to the farmer, the cook, and the others who had helped to make my eating possible. And finally, with that one forkful of food still hanging in front of me, I'd become aware that if my thumb wasn't positioned just as it is, or my elbow didn't have the mobility it does, I wouldn't be able to complete the act, and that led me into gratitude for the wonder of a functioning body. But my body works in ways that go beyond the mechanical. As I put the food between my lips at last, I experience the texture of the food, and its taste, and also the pleasure it gives me. By this point, I'm sitting at the table awed by the multiple wonders that are tied up in this simple, daily action. It strikes me that every act of my life embodies such complexity, interdependence, and mystery, and that it's up to me whether I call out a blessing to name and give thanks for all these gifts, or whether I just boorishly guzzle and chew.

But Luzzatto tells us there's still a catch, because even if we are successful in separating ourselves from negative influences and then bringing a spirit of sanctity to our deeds, there is still no guarantee that we will arrive at a state of holiness. While it's not likely that holiness will arise in us *unless* we prepare ourselves, if it *should* come, it will be only as an act of divine grace through a process we can only influence, not control. But it seems to me that just by doing what we can to prepare to be gifted with holiness, we will be improving our lives. That in itself is a gift—something we can give to ourselves and to those around us.

True to the Mussar tradition, Rabbi Perr had deftly melded the elevated notion of holiness with practical realism about this life as it is. So, toward the end of our time together that day, I couldn't resist pushing a little further by asking him about Luzzatto's suggestion that those who are of the most exalted purity and saintliness can reach an even more sublime potential—being given "the keys to the resurrection of the dead."

Of course, I had seen in the daily prayers that it is written, "You are mighty forever, my God; You resurrect the dead." And I knew that this whole issue is deeply rooted in Jewish thought, going back to the Bible and being prominent in medieval sources. But was this an idea to be taken literally? For me, the idea that the dead can be brought back to life is just too fantastic. But with the doctrine of resurrection plunked right there at the very summit of the Mussar mountain, how could I just turn away? Would I be satisfied to plant my flag on the ridge of holiness, about two hundred yards short of the peak? Was resurrection really the ultimate goal of the path I was tracking?

Rabbi Perr's answer came quickly. "There is enough good in that book without coming to the end of it," he said. "Resurrection's another conversation, but for now, if we could revive the dead who are *ourselves,* the living dead, that would be sufficient." Then he smiled one of his crinkly-eyed smiles, the wrinkles radiating all the way to his temples.

I stood reminded. The focus of Mussar is on ourselves in this life. We might be lured into tantalizing speculation about the foggy future, but where would that get us? Our job is to focus on sanctifying every one of our actions right down here on earth, so that we will be prepared to receive the gift of holiness that is our highest potential, should it be offered.

The way Mussar explains it, being holy doesn't mean becoming anything other than human. It just means becoming the ultimate version of a human that one can be. The goal Mussar sets for us is summarized in that marvelous Yiddish word *mensch.* To be a *mensch* is to carry the fullest measure of the integrity, goodness, and honor a person can hope for in this life. Put in these terms, Mussar is a path of *"mensch-*making." Rabbi Salanter speaks in one place about this way of seeing Mussar: "The Maharal of Prague created a *golem* [a fantastic supernatural creature of Jewish folklore] and this was a great wonder," he wrote. "But how much more wonderful is it to transform a corporeal human being into a *mensch.*"

OPENING THE GATE

USING MENTAL IMAGES AND
CONTEMPLATION TO GAIN INSIGHT

One of the principal forms of Mussar practice is guided contemplation. In *The Duties of the Heart*, Bahya ibn Pakuda tells us that in this practice we use our imagination to imprint understanding directly on our hearts because vivid mental images etch chosen messages directly on the soul. The intellect is not the most profound aspect of the soul; it is not the root. But impressions—wholesome as well as unwholesome—gathered in the mind do pass down to the root, and color and shape the soul.

One of the contemplations ibn Pakuda gives us is intended to help us enhance the trait of humility. Humility gets a lot of attention in Mussar because it is the inner quality that is ranked as the primary prerequisite for holiness. Without humility, we might be too proud to acknowledge our other weaknesses, and so we wouldn't be inclined to work so hard to make the necessary inner changes. An inflated ego surrounds us with a barrier truth cannot penetrate. It is an obstacle to making progress on any of the other soul-traits that might need improvement.

Rabbi Rafael of Barshad, a nineteenth-century European teacher, points out how we tend to be arrogant even when we don't have very much substance on which to hang that pride. "When I get to heaven," he said, "they'll ask me, why didn't you learn more Torah? And I'll tell them that I'm slow-witted. Then they'll ask me, why didn't you do more kindnesses for others? And I'll tell them that I'm physically weak. Then they'll ask me, why didn't you give more to charity? And I'll tell them that I didn't have enough money. But then they'll ask me: if you were so stupid, weak, and poor, why were you so arrogant? And for that I won't have an answer."

To strengthen the soul-trait of humility, ibn Pakuda directs us to walk the mind slowly and methodically along the full journey of life, from the fertilization of the egg all the way through death and decay. This guided contemplation, which I've included below, leads us to an awareness that the order of the world cannot in any way be credited to human invention, and engenders great appreciation for the wisdom of the divine. It leads us to an understanding of how kind and generous God is toward us, and this insight fosters a healthy and genuine sense of humility and gratitude for all we have received.

Many Mussar sources tell us to fix a specific time every day to do practice, and I have found this to be a useful discipline because it sidesteps the issue of whether or not I feel like doing it that day. I've found evenings to be a good time for me, and chances are that it's just those evenings when I feel least like learning and reflecting that I have the most to gain from study and review. In preparation, I spend a few minutes of silence just bringing my mind into focus before directing my conscious thought to the words of ibn Pakuda's practice. (I've actually expanded upon his description in order to make the contemplation more thorough.) When my mind has become quiet enough to listen deeply, I begin.

"Reflect on how generous God has been to man: how [God] created the womb as a sort of crib for man's use at his inception, so he would be in a safe, well-guarded fortress where no one could touch him, and

where he would be unaffected by hot or cold, where he is well-shielded, encased, protected, and provided with nourishment. It is there, in a place no one else can get to, that he grows and develops, moves about, and eats effortlessly."

Fully grown in the womb, the baby emerges. Birth is an amazing, mysterious process where, usually at just the right time, the mother's body delivers a new human being into the world. It seems impossible that a seven- or eight-pound baby could fit through the tiny birth canal, but that miracle happens daily, and is provided for. Nicely greased to ease the passage, the baby emerges. Every time, a mystery!

In the beginning, the infant is entirely dependent on others, especially the mother, who provides food from her own body. But in time the little muscles grow, the consciousness forms, and a child begins to differentiate. Tentative and wobbly at first, steps soon lead to reckless running, riding, jumping, climbing. With each day, cells multiply and growth happens. Illness and accidents happen, too. Learning is taking place.

Contemplate all the organs that have been set into the body to permit us to do all that we do in life: the heart and veins, the lungs, the eyes and ears, the nose . . . all complex, all coordinated, all doing their jobs like a well-trained crew.

We grow, we mature, we learn. We find our work. Another round of the cycle is initiated as we pass through adolescence to become adults, perhaps to bear our own children.

We excel. We stumble and fall. We laugh. We cry. This is life.

And through it all, time passes and we age. The children grow through their own cycles. We mature in our occupations and activities and no longer feel the same driving needs that moved us to action earlier. Our bodies slowly age too, cell by cell.

Our time is limited, and we are nearing the limit. It happens to everyone. It is the way. And then we die. One day, some day, each of us takes a last breath.

"Notice how suddenly, unwittingly, without warning, and randomly other beings, sentient and nonsentient alike, die. Notice too that there is not a single month of the year when death does not come, nor is there a day of the month or an hour of the day when it cannot; and that it does not necessarily come in old age rather than middle age, young adulthood, youth, childhood, or infancy, for it can happen anytime and anyplace.

"It is as if a king left collateral with you without declaring when you should return it, and he ordered you to expect him to reappear at any time and to thus go nowhere, but to be available all the time for his visit."

Why should this frighten us? This is how it is. This is the cycle that is given to us. Nothing does not have an end, and we are no exception. Behind our closed eyes, we see the vastness of space and hear the quiet of eternity.

When, after a few more minutes, I open my eyes, I'm still there, but I see things a little bit differently. This contemplation awakens an accurate and honest insight into our place in the great scheme of things. Although the wonder of life is before our eyes all our waking days, we are usually asleep to its profound truth. Through these mental images, we arouse a deep and humbling awareness of the reality of our existence, and if we have heard it deeply enough, it gets inscribed in the soul.

CHAPTER FIVE

THE GATE OF
GOOD AND EVIL

*"A man [is] sitting in front of two roads, one com-
mencing among thorns and running into a plain, the
other starting in a plain and leading into thorns, and
he advises the wayfarer and says: 'See you the way
with thorns at the beginning, after a few steps it will
lead you into a plain, but the road with the plain at
the start will soon lead you among the thorns.' It is so
with the way of righteousness and the way of wickedness. Do not be dismayed by the difficult start, but
choose the way that in the end leads to eternal life."*

— THE TALMUD

I've always assumed, as I suspect most of us do, that, with the
notable exceptions of murderers, psychopaths, child abusers,
and the like, humankind is inherently inclined to do good,
and to be the best we can be. And Mussar teaches that as well.
At the heart of Mussar is the belief that, because we are all
created in God's image, we are inherently pure. Goodness is

expected of us, even though layers of ignorance, unresolved experience, and habit might sometimes hide that innate virtue.

But if we accept that our inborn nature inclines us to do good, why are there so many apparently moral, respectable, and responsible people who do bad, destructive—one might even say evil—deeds, or who knowingly engage in activities that damage either themselves or others? For Mussar, the answer lies in a force called the *yetzer ha-ra*, which we all know because it appears to us as that niggling, irrepressible voice that lives in each of us, whose sole purpose is to drive us to do things that are not in the best interest of the soul—our own or someone else's.

The *yetzer ha-ra* is the dastardly opponent to our efforts to elevate and improve our inner qualities, and anyone can fall victim to its wiles. Even when we have grown in our awareness and mastery over our inner traits, Mussar warns, the *yetzer ha-ra* remains on the prowl, watching for an unguarded moment in which to pounce and send us sprawling.

When I look back on my own business downfall, it's not hard for me to see the handiwork of the *yetzer ha-ra*. I can pinpoint just how I succumbed to those insistent whisperings that preyed on my ambitions and my ego: "Go on! Do it! This is how . . ." But that doesn't mean I'm not responsible. On the contrary, it was I who listened to those whisperings and obeyed. When tempted, I allowed myself to be led astray, and I'm sure I made the *yetzer ha-ra* very happy.

The Mussar teachers acknowledge that we all also possess a *yetzer ha-tov*—an urge to do good—but they haven't spent nearly as much time concerned with this positive impulse. Our inherent nature is good, they say, and if it weren't for the sordid forces operating in the world and in us, our compass would naturally swing toward the good.

Mussar sources tell us that the *yetzer ha-ra* does its work by closing the heart and disconnecting us from a life of soul; and so, if I hoped to get anywhere on Mussar's path, I needed to gain a thorough understanding of this, my prime inner adversary.

I t was when I poked my head into Rabbi Perr's office for the second time one day that he motioned me inside and indicated he had a few minutes to spare. I could hear muffled voices from the adjoining study hall in the background and asked him whether he had a little spy window that allowed the sounds to come through so clearly. He laughed and showed me a space where the old joint between the walls that separated the two rooms had given way. When he had returned to his chair, and turned his eyes to me, I asked him simply, "The *yetzer ha-ra*?"

At that his smile evaporated, for there is no more serious issue than our drive toward evil. He picked up a piece of paper from his desk, studied it for a moment while he thought, then set it down. With eyes still cast downward, he began his answer. "The simplest understanding of *yetzer ha-ra* is based on the saying of the sages: 'If we didn't call it a name, we wouldn't be able to cope with it.'" Now looking my way, he asked rhetorically, "Why? Because if a person sees the consistent wrong in himself as *himself,* he has no motivation to fight it. It's as if he were saying, 'I have met the *yetzer ha-ra* and it's me, so what's there to talk about?'" He let that idea hang in the air for a moment, then explained more simply. "In order to cope with it and to see it as evil, it has to be projected outside the self.

"However," he quickly added, introducing a new line of

thought, "in the Talmud it says 'It's all the same, the *yetzer ha-ra*, Satan, and the Angel of Death.' And that," he said, leaning forward, a gleam in his eye, dropping his voice almost to a whisper, "brings up an immensely interesting topic."

Now he sat back in his chair. "As I get older, it is illustrated to me over and over again that we are our own worst enemy, and perhaps our only enemy, and that is expressed in a physical as well as a spiritual sense. How many of us smoke or overeat?" At that point, he glanced down at his own rounded belly. "Also guilty to a degree," he grimaced.

"Even the man who runs for his health to the point where he ruins his knees and ankles, he is also his own worst enemy, because, in trying to help himself, he is not a moderate person.

"A lot of the time, what causes our problems with our competitors, our neighbors, whoever, is really that we don't have the right attitude. We don't know how to accept a problem or respond to a problem, so we are our own worst enemy. With the proper attitude, even death and cancer would not be enemies. But the right attitude," he reflected, "that requires a lifetime of cultivation.

"But just because developing the right attitude helps," he hastened to add, "that doesn't mean evil doesn't exist. Yes, Virginia, there really *is* evil! It can merge with a human personality and take over, like some alien creature in control of a person, and a person's whole personality is eaten up until there is nothing left of him and he becomes totally evil. It's like a destructive fire, and the person who is immersed in it has to face that fire eventually.

"Why should evil have so much power? There can be several hundred people milling about, and one person yells, 'Lynch him,' and suddenly they are all united with one goal—to break into the jail and grab this guy and hang him. They're all caught up in it and they become a mob. Have you ever seen a mob do anything good? Never! To do something good, there will first be a committee and then a debate—about what is good, how to do it, should it be done, aren't there better ways to do it. Evil is like a virus—it's easy to catch it. It's hard to catch good health, but it's easy to catch illness.

"I don't doubt that there is such a thing as evil, that there is such a thing as Satan and the *yetzer ha-ra*. He is seductive, he gets a hand on people, and he destroys them." He growled out these last words. "All of us contain evil; it just depends on the choices we make."

Mussar isn't the kind of discipline that invites us to bury our heads in the sand in happy-go-lucky denial. On the contrary, it insists that evil is real, it is out there, and, although some may personify it as Satan or the Devil, what we really need to be concerned about is evil that runs like a dark stream in every human heart, including yours and mine. It appears to us as that conniving, self-serving little voice that daily whispers in our ear, and that we have so much trouble resisting. The Talmud warns us: "First the Evil Impulse is like a passerby, then he is called a guest, and finally he becomes master of the house." Mussar practice helps us to recognize and resist negative impulses within ourselves—and to make changes in ourselves so there will be less to resist.

With the increased self-awareness that Mussar induces, I now see that I encounter the *yetzer ha-ra* on a daily basis. It's that little voice encouraging me to be lazy. Or to work obsessively late into the night without taking the time to read my daughters a bedtime story. I've sworn off coffee because I know it gives me wild swings of mood and energy, and it's the *yetzer ha-ra* that's urging me to have just one cup, even though I know full well the price I'll have to pay.

If we hope to contend with the *yetzer ha-ra,* we need to understand how it operates, and that is by falsehood. It doesn't say to us, "Here, do this, it's really bad," because that would give away its game. So instead it says, "Here, do this, it's really good," even though it's inviting us to ruin.

There is a story about a Jewish sage who was already an elderly and highly revered man. When he would wake up in the morning, a little voice would say to him, "You know, you are already such an accomplished and well-respected person. You've achieved so much in one life. Why don't you give yourself just ten more minutes of sleep. It's still so early." To which the sage would reply, "It can't be so early if *you're* already up."

Its masquerade may be effective and its promises convincing, but the urgings of the *yetzer ha-ra* are always bogus. It is so wily that it can even twist our good instincts to its own ends. When the soul sends us sound guidance, the *yetzer ha-ra* is likely to pipe up and warn us not to listen to that alien voice making those absurd demands. It tries to harden our hearts to the needs and pain of others, and in the same way, it also tries to close our ears even to the wisdom that lies within us. Its whole job is to mislead us so that we will give priority to the less real instead of what is ultimately true.

While the *yetzer ha-ra* features in each one of us, it is not generally considered to be an aspect of the soul. Rather, it is described as an innate attribute of human nature that has more vitality than a soul-trait because it is a dynamic force—just like its opposite, the urge to do good, the *yetzer ha-tov*. An analogy I have found useful for explaining these opposing forces is that the soul-traits are like the volume and station settings on your radio tuner. They remain in the same positions whether the radio is turned on or off. But it is only when you turn the radio on, introducing a dynamic force into the system—electricity in the radio or one of the *yetzers* in our lives—that the levels of the settings are expressed.

Since everything ultimately comes from God, so must the *yetzer ha-ra*. But for millennia, people have been asking why God would have implanted such a will to do evil in people. Rabbi Perr's answer is that it is "something to surmount. It is something to teach us. It guides us."

The *yetzer ha-ra* is our guide because it has the uncanny ability to reveal just those places where our heart is most vulnerable to the lure of desire. If we are vain, it will prey on our vanity; if we are miserly, it will try to convince us that we had better hold on to what we've got. In this way, it serves us by showing up just those soul-traits we need to address if we hope to edge our way toward holiness. And it provides us with a more than worthy opponent against which to test ourselves and develop our spiritual strength.

"But," warns Rabbi Perr, "if given too much leeway, and let out of the box, it's a tiger that destroys everything around it. God created the *yetzer ha-ra*, but he also created ways of overcoming it, if you only trust Him. Many will fall, but it is there to provide us with choice, as a way of discovering who is the one who will conquer."

So, despite its siren call, it is not inevitable that we follow the *yetzer ha-ra*. Our work is to tame it by strengthening our will to resist, affirming commitments we will not breach, and erecting barriers against temptations to evil which will be different for each of us, according to the state of our individual soul.

The *yetzer ha-ra* works by fanning the flames of desire. The entire Mussar system of Rabbi Israel Salanter rests on the idea that the human impulse to do harm has but one root: human appetite. Salanter, as a leader of Orthodox Jews, was concerned because desire for sensual pleasure leads to the transgression of the traditional laws and commandments. Nowhere does he even hint that pleasure, in and of itself, is evil, but he helpfully draws our attention to the power of craving to make us act in ways that ultimately cause suffering. Buddhism also contains this insight, seeing all human suffering as arising from desire, and Rabbi Perr summed up contemporary culture along much the same lines: "The big issue today is materialism, because materialism eats up spirituality. It's very hard to have both. America is a country of appetites."

Almost any discussion of the *yetzer ha-ra* inevitably leads to the question of "sin." And it is sin that the Mussar literature warns us about. After all, if we are being lured away from the path of goodness, or holiness, we must be heading the opposite way—toward sin. But what a difficult word that has become! Does the notion of sin even retain any value in a world where most things that might conventionally have been labeled sinful are now considered simply lifestyle choices? It's an especially tricky idea in a pluralistic society that rejects any one group's imposing its morality on another.

When I asked Rabbi Perr about this, he answered, "Sin is out of style today. We almost have to apologize for the concept, because in a secular world there is no sin. For some people, there seems to be no difference between my doing something wrong and a tiger attacking a lamb. To these people, that is certainly not wrong, because it's what a tiger does. So sin is not something that is easily understood in our times."

He was pointing to the increasing tendency to assign human failings to biological and physiological sources. If our behavior is determined by our genetic makeup, are we any less pre-programmed than a tiger? And are we any more responsible? Rabbi Perr and the Mussar tradition would answer emphatically that we have infinitely more free will than any other animal, and we hold responsibility in direct proportion to that.

"Sometimes we are not aware of the wrong that we do," he went on. "Sometimes we just discover later on how wrong we were, how wrongheaded, and it is so overwhelming that we are left breathless. The word in Hebrew for sin happens to be the same as the word for 'missing a mark' or 'missing a goal.' This makes sin not something you've *done* but something you've *missed,* something you've misconstrued. It isn't a criticism of you as a person, or something that should be associated with guilt."

"But," he continued, gazing at me intently over his glasses and bracing the palms of his hands on his desktop, "I bridle at the idea of soft-pedaling something that is a sin. Sin means having done wrong, and not only is sin wrong, but there is a very serious concern that sin contaminates the rest of us, the totality of humanity. One sinner can contaminate other people, that we know. It must be recognized that sin has a profound effect on the individual and the rest of humanity." And then, coming around to end his comments on a hopeful note, as he always did, he added, "But it can be purged. One of the finest purgings, and valid, is to go ahead and do good things, which is wonderful."

But what is this thing called "sin" that we are purging? I want the word "sin" to describe that deep sense we can sometimes have that something is just not healthy or nourishing to the soul, and that acts as a signal to avoid just those things. I have heard sin defined as "spiritual mediocrity" and that rings true for me. But that same word, sin, appears to me to be loaded with danger because it is such a convenient weapon for any authoritarian or fanatical cleric who wants to target anyone labeled as "different." I believe there are lines we should not cross because the result would be suffering and contamination of ourselves and those around us. Using that as a definition, I can know when I have sinned. And yet the problem still remains unresolved for me— that this useful spiritual word is so easily co-opted by servants of coercive, power-wielding organizations as a means of persecution.

In the time that I have known him, Rabbi Perr has been anything but judgmental toward me, nor has he ever tried to coerce me into taking on Orthodox ways. Once, in fact, he sat me down to tell me that I shouldn't feel pressured to do everything their way, just because I was present in their world. But I know, too, that he has inherited a traditional understanding of the label "sin," and his understanding is not anywhere near as liberal—or confused—as mine. This was an instance where I found that I came at life from a different viewpoint, and where my ideas just didn't mesh with the Orthodox worldview.

But where our paths reconverge is in the way we see the faculty of conscience as a helpful guide to action. "There is a saying," Rabbi Perr quoted, "that 'we only appoint to public office someone who has a serious flaw in his past.' Now, I've said 'serious flaw,' " he explained, "but the actual phrase the sages use is 'a basket of worms and bugs.' Unless he has a basket of worms and bugs hanging on his back, we can't appoint him to public office."

He gave out a long, savoring chuckle, and then proclaimed, "This is wise, because a good person who has had a serious breach is going to be very careful. He doesn't want to go through the pain and the healing of that sort of breach again.

"How important it is," Rabbi Perr went on, "to listen to that inner voice. How important it is to listen to your conscience."

Even in a world as structured and dominated by rules as Orthodoxy, in the end, we are told, a voice heard within us will help guide our steps. And when we make mistakes, when we stray, *when we sin,* the prick of conscience is there to act as a source of further guidance. Our knowledge of what nurtures the soul, our awareness of the lines beyond which lie pain and suffering, our appreciation of conscience, are natural to us and can be cultivated. Experience can help us develop these qualities. Experience will also help us learn to discern the helpful inner voice from the other one, and to grow comfortable with following the guidance that nurtures the soul.

That brings us to another fundamental Mussar truth related to the concepts of good and evil—that we are able to change, to develop our positive soul-traits, and to choose to do good because we have *free will.* "The moral powers are not predetermined, for man has freedom of will to choose his course in life," the Talmud affirms. And if this were not so, Mussar would have no reason to exist, because there would be no course of change for us to undertake.

Because we have free will, we determine the fate of our souls. It is up to us to choose to bring virtue or evil into the world, and we play an enormous role in creating or avoiding suffering, for ourselves and for others. If we believe in divine justice, the wages of sin are damnation. But if we don't, there's a good chance we will be paying—or collecting the rewards—for our actions right here in this life.

"I can't believe that all of us can't get better," Rabbi Perr said to me at the end of that day. "I just don't believe it. Mussar doesn't believe it. Torah doesn't believe it. The Rambam [Maimonides] said something about this I want to read to you . . ." And with that he got up, hurried out of the room, and returned a few minutes later holding a large open book, from which he translated for me. " 'Let it not pass through your mind like the fools of the non-Jews and most of the stupid Jews'—here he calls it a *'golem.'* A *golem* is like a . . . a . . . ." He reached for a translation. Finally he shrugged his shoulders and exclaimed: "A *golem!*" Then he continued with the explanation that it is only fools like these who believe " '. . . that God decrees from the time he is created whether [a man] will be a holy person or an evil-doer. That is not correct. He could be wise or stupid, or merciful or cruel, or cheap or generous, and so all the other qualities.' "

He looked up at me then, still holding the book. "The reason he says 'don't let it pass through your mind' is because it's so easy to give up. But it's not decreed, any of these things. Holiness and evil are not decreed. We have choice."

So, if we all have a choice, and if we are all good at the core, how do we come to do evil? By acting in ways that we might not if only we were as aware as we could be. Awareness is the first line of resistance to the *yetzer ha-ra*. When the mind is not trained to be aware, it tends to get sucked into the swirling torrents of emotion and knee-jerk reactions that spring up in response to whatever happens in our life. As a result, too often our lives are directed by unnoticed interior states and unrecognized ways of being. Mussar wakes us up to the tyranny of negative impulses so that we can take steps to give ourselves more room in which to exercise our freedom of choice. In Rabbi Perr's terms, the practice teaches us how to open up a little space between the match and the fuse. Instead of being catapulted blindly in a random direction by an automatic response to something that pushes one of our buttons, we foster awareness, and so gift ourselves with the spaciousness to choose the course that is good for the soul.

OPENING THE GATE

DEVELOPING SELF-AWARENESS

Mussar tells us that our efforts at change depend on first knowing ourself thoroughly, accurately, and honestly; and so, over the centuries, the Mussar masters have developed effective methods just for the purpose of bringing us to an awareness of what lives in the depths of our soul.

AWARENESS PRACTICE 1:
Heshbon ha-Nefesh
(An Accounting of the Soul)

One of the best awareness practices I have found is called *heshbon ha-nefesh*, which means, literally, "the accounting of the soul." This technique for inner scrutiny is not the product of a twentieth-century psychologist or a California self-help guru, but of nineteenth-century Eastern European Orthodox Jewish thinking. It was first laid out in 1812 by an insightful rabbi named Menachem Mendel Leffin of Satanow.

Rabbi Leffin's practice is a way to work at improving thirteen soul-traits over the course of a year. You work intensively on only one *middah* per week, so that over the course of fifty-two weeks you will have gone through the full roster of thirteen a total of four times. In other words, in that year you will have spent four weeks working on each of your priority traits.

This sort of repetitive cycle is typical of the Mussar approach. Rabbi Perr explained: "That's the traditional way. It is impossible to keep focusing on the same *middah* over and over and over again endlessly, because it just wears you down. You can burn your brains out by working on one thing constantly." Never wanting to dwell on the negative, he went on: "But beside the fact that it is just not practical to go forever on just one *middah*, it's true that once a person gets the bug for bettering himself, working on one thing enhances another. People learn to like the idea of making things better."

The first stage of this practice requires that you identify the thirteen traits you want to work on. This is done by keeping a special notebook in which to record all of the actions and thoughts that in some way reveal something about your own soul-traits. As you make notes on what you see cropping up in your daily life, it shouldn't take more than a week or two to recognize that certain traits are showing up with a lot more regularity than others; these are the ones to put on your list of thirteen. This diary-keeping works as a kind of scorecard, and Rabbi Leffin encourages us to tally up the days when we "blew it" in each area. I've found, however, that rather than simply toting up numbers, it gives me more insight to write out briefly the actual details of the events themselves.

We are supposed to do this at the end of each day, and so, to begin the practice, I put my notebook next to my bed and, just before going to sleep, I would look back over my day and write down any incidents I could recall that reflected anything about any of my soul-traits. When did I speak harshly or kindly? Truthfully or not so? When did I think a greedy or jealous thought? When was I lazy or energetic? After doing this for a while, I was able to compose my original list of thirteen traits, which included, in no particular order of priority: equanimity; surrender; trust in God; truth in speech; compassion; humility; awe of heaven; zeal; loving-kindness; concentration; abstinence; dignity; courage.

To show you how this works, here are some journal selections that made me aware that "truth in speech" belonged on my list:

I attended a lecture at the university given by someone whom I had known as a graduate student. Since then, he has continued in academia while I long ago wandered off. At lunch, he sat opposite me, and early in the conversation he asked what I thought of a particular

*book. I had read it years before and couldn't recall a thing about it
except title and author. I hemmed and hawed until he came out with
his opinion (which was actually what I think he wanted to do anyway). Why couldn't I just have been honest and said, "To tell you the
truth, I don't remember a thing about it"?*

*The phone rang. I checked the call display gizmo and saw that it
was the bank. I knew immediately what it was about—some forms I
had not got around to signing—so I didn't take the call. I had to go
out in the afternoon anyway, so I planned to go by the bank. When I
did stop in, the clerk told me she had phoned me just that morning.
"Really?" I said. "What a coincidence!" It was a lie, a small lie.*

*I was walking the dog one day soon after a big windstorm. I met
a neighbor and we stopped to chat. "You know," I said, "I saw two cars
that had been smashed by trees." In truth, I had seen one car with its
windshield shattered. The other car I had been told about. I caught
myself, and with what seemed like tortured mental effort, I forced my
jaws to utter, "Actually, I saw one and heard about the other."*

These selections sit in my notebook like stiff corpses on the
battlefield of my moral life. Each one had a different underlying
cause—in the first I think I was fearful of losing face before an
esteemed colleague; in the last I was just exaggerating for effect—but when I recorded the third one, I could no longer ignore the fact that verbal honesty (or lack thereof) was showing
up with too much regularity; clearly it belonged on my list of
traits to work on.

After I came up with my thirteen traits, I was ready to move
on to the next stage of the practice, which is to write a one-line

summary of each of the traits we have chosen to work on. Rabbi Leffin provides some samples. For "truth" he writes, "Do not allow anything to pass your lips that you are not certain is completely true." For "equanimity" he suggests, "Rise above events that are inconsequential—both bad and good—for they are not worth disturbing your equanimity." And so on. We can use his summary statements, or we can compose our own.

In the morning, before beginning our day, we are to read to ourselves the summary statement pertaining to the trait we are working on that week. Then, in the evening, we record in our diary anything that happened during the day that relates only to that same trait. So, in the morning, we affirm to ourselves the ideal we are seeking, and at night, we see how well we have done.

That's the whole practice. It seems so minimal, but what these directions don't reveal is the impact the *heshbon ha-nefesh* practice can have on raising our level of self-awareness moment-to-moment. It does this by directing us to be watchful for inner fault lines as they are revealed in the small tremors of everyday life. This, in turn, helps us to identify, and ultimately address, the pressures and fractures that exist beneath the surface of consciousness before they erupt in shattering earthquakes.

Some evenings early on, I would search my mind for incidents where my speech, or my body, or my thoughts revealed aspects of who I am, and I would just draw a blank. Anything I had experienced that didn't have some sort of bright marker attached to it had apparently been instantly erased from my memory bank. But with time, I found that I had something to note every night, as the tentacles of this practice imperceptibly invaded all my experiences throughout the day, and I involuntarily began to pay more attention to what was happening in my life.

For example, I'd find myself driving along, and when I would make some aggressive move with the car, my mind would immediately pipe up, "Better remember that tonight." Or I would say something that wasn't exactly true, and in my mind a little guy in striped overalls would march out and plant a flag right beside my words as they lay there still steaming fresh on the field of memory.

I even began to catch sight of thoughts and feelings as they were taking shape, and on some occasions this helped me to stop myself from doing or saying something I knew I would later regret. These changes were all the direct result of the sharpened awareness that is the intended effect of this practice.

But how does awareness like this ultimately impact the soul-traits on our list? In my case, I've described how I came to put "truth in speech" on my own list, but the transgressions I noted were tiny, weren't they? No one really got hurt. So why make such a big fuss about it? The answer, of course, is that even though there may have been no obvious victim in these situations, if I could allow the truth to slide so easily on a trivial, daily basis, how reliable would I be—to myself and to others—when life pitched me a really hard curve? How tempted would I be to fudge the truth then, and what might be the consequences? Well, I already knew the answer to that one, because lack of truthfulness had been so significant in the failure of my business. This Mussar practice was opening my eyes to a trait of character that really did need some serious work. And yet, without my regularly recording them, I suspect that each of these incidents might have slipped under the radar of my awareness.

The intention in this practice, of course, is not to line up all your failures and then to beat yourself up over them, because that just can't be a positive step for the soul. The central point is really to reveal to consciousness the contents of the unconscious mind. These are, by definition, hidden from us, and so no matter how hard we peer directly into our inner selves, we won't uncover anything of what lurks below the surface. But because the contents of our unconscious are perfectly reflected in the patterns of our deeds, certain images return night after night, and the patterns become unmistakable. We need this truth about ourselves to guide our steps on the path to deep, lasting, fulfilling transformation. And, in fact, as soon as we have brought to light those soul-traits that might otherwise have continued to live in darkness, we have already begun to change.

AWARENESS PRACTICE 2:
Behira Points
(Learning from the Choices We Make)

Another way that Mussar helps us to identify soul-traits we need to work on is by directing us to reflect systematically on the actual *choices* we make in our daily lives. Examining those choices holds up a magnifying glass to our soul-traits in action. If we then focus on those choices that are most problematic for us, or for those around us, we will be able to develop a clear picture of the areas within us that call for greatest attention. One person's problem might be gambling, another's might be overeating, and a third person might have a problem making enough time for a partner or family. Wherever your own challenge might come, it will be just where your own soul is calling out for growth or healing.

Rabbi Eliyahu Dessler, a disciple of the Slobodka school

of Mussar and one of the great Mussar masters of the mid-twentieth century, illustrates this truth by comparing the approaches of two people to the issue of whether or not to steal. One man is born into a family of thieves, so for him, robbery is a way of life and isn't perceived as an ethical issue. The other is born to a strict, upright, learned family. He has never been tempted to steal, and therefore robbery is not an ethical issue for him either. And yet, each of these people will still confront areas where free will becomes a challenge, where choices have to be made. The committed thief might agonize over whether or not to shoot his way out of a jam. He would steal without hesitation, but would he murder? The honest man, on the other hand, might struggle over the amount he gives to charity or whether he is giving in the right, generous spirit. When we are able to pinpoint those places where choice becomes an issue for us, we will have identified our most crucial and vital thresholds for growth and healing.

These are called, in Hebrew, *behira* points, because the word *behira* translates into English as "free will." The points where we are challenged will be unique to each of us, and may be located in any area of our lives, but they aren't usually difficult to locate if we are willing to take an honest and reflective look at our own behavior and the choices we make. Where we feel or cause pain is a big clue, because, since we tend to be creatures of habit, our most important *behira* points are often associated with repeated problems, and they are usually problems that bring suffering to ourselves and to others.

Try it. Think back over the past couple of days and consider what decisions and choices you made. Select one incident and focus in on it. There may be some pain associated with this incident, but don't let that make you turn away because it's a good indication that you've located a soul-trait that needs work. What qualities did you bring to making that choice: were you decisive, impulsive, timid, calm? What were your motives? Were you generous, greedy, vengeful, caring? What emotions surrounded the decision? Equanimity? Agitation? Pain? Happiness? Worry?

As you go through these investigations, you will see reflections of your very own soul-traits cast on the screen of your life. The details are important, so don't be hasty. And don't be tempted either to praise or berate yourself for the decisions you made. Your job here is simply to be honest, and to confirm for yourself the areas where you have the option to exercise free will, the opportunity to opt for the higher over the less virtuous. You are seeking the precious gift of insight to identify those places where, with a little effort, you could elevate yourself one notch closer to being the person you already are in your pure depths.

CHAPTER SIX

THE GATE OF
FEAR OF GOD

"The end of the matter, all having been heard: fear God and keep His commandments, for this is the whole of man."

— ECCLESIASTES 12:13,

QUOTED IN THE FIRST LINE

OF *ORCHOS TZADIKKIM*

A s I became more familiar with Mussar, its concepts and vocabulary became a part of my everyday life. Even discordant notions like "sin" began to find a place in my thinking, although my understanding might not have been as traditional and conservative as Rabbi Perr's. But among the many concepts I had to learn and interpret for myself, there was one that I tripped over every time I came upon it, and I found I came across it often. The Mussar sources—including Rabbi Perr—are unanimous in saying that fear of God—*yirat hashamayim,* literally "fear of heaven"—is an essential attitude that all seekers must cultivate. That was a very tough concept for me to swallow and digest.

Whenever I thought about a fearsome God, all that came to mind were Hollywood-style images of that terrifying, patriarchal, fulminating, punishing intercessor of the Old Testament. And even if I did manage to put aside Charlton Heston on the mountaintop, I still didn't grasp why the Mussar teachers gave such heavy emphasis to developing this attitude. Rabbi Perr had repeatedly stated his belief in the literal truth of divine retribution, yet fear seemed almost the polar opposite of what I felt I wanted to cultivate in myself. Love, certainly, but fear?

Yet fear of God is a recurring theme in both the Torah and the Talmud, and it is braided like a strand of indestructible titanium into the central cable of the Mussar tradition. "And now, O Israel, what does HaShem your God ask of you but to fear HaShem your God?" the Torah exhorts us. And in Ecclesiastes we are told, "HaShem has wrought so that men should fear Him."

In the Talmud, Rava says, "When a man is brought to judgment, he is asked: 'Were you honest in your dealings, did you set aside times for Torah study, did you engage in procreation, did you aspire to salvation, were you dialectical in wisdom, did you understand one thing from another?' And even if he did [all or none of these things], if fear of HaShem is his treasure, he emerges meritorious in judgment, and if not, not."

What made this notion even harder for me is the fact we are told that it is up to us to *choose*, of our own free will, to fear God. I had no idea why I would want to do that. I simply couldn't see any spiritual benefit to be gained from adopting a fearful mind-state, and what I really wanted to do was reject the whole idea as just a relic of primitive thinking held over from another time; but, of course, when I put that idea to Rabbi Perr, he was not about to let me off the hook so easily.

"I realize that history is not a straight road," he said. "History turns, and if you don't turn with it, you're not going to be on the road very long, you're going to run smack into a tree. I am aware of that. Even so, I am not interested in any phony baloney, that people take what they wish, pick and choose, and make it up as they go along. I don't feel it's legitimate. It's not authentic."

To his mind, Mussar—and all of Jewish tradition—is not like a fruit salad, where you get to eat the apples and peaches and whatever else suits your taste, and leave the grapes behind. So, did that mean it was time for me to learn to quake and tremble?

I was at home with Rabbi and Mrs. Perr one afternoon, enjoying one of those long and rambling conversations I sometimes got to share with them, although we were continually interrupted by the ringing of the telephone. Most callers asked practical questions about the yeshiva or about the summer program run by Mrs. Perr. More than a few were concerned parents on the everlasting quest for suitable marriage partners for their children. Some were people seeking help with difficult ethical problems, such as the woman who wanted to know how she could advise a friend not to send her child to a particular playgroup without revealing her confidential knowledge that the husband of the playgroup leader was suspected of some impropriety. The caller wanted to protect the child without breaching a trust.

"I'll call you back," Mrs. Perr told her, and immediately the three of us descended on the problem like a SWAT team on a hostage-taking. Until the next phone call came. This was ethics in action, Mussar at work in the field of life, and I loved every minute of it. It helped that, as each question or problem came up, Rabbi and Mrs. Perr wanted to know what I thought, too. I had been so nervous when I first met them, because I didn't know how they would receive me and I was fearful that I would make stupidly obvious mistakes as I stumbled through their highly structured world. And I did make gaffes—like carrying my *tefillin* to the yeshiva on a Saturday, and talking at moments when silence is the rule at the table—but they never criticized or condemned me. If they said anything, it was always by way of patient guidance. Once, as I sat reading at their house while waiting for Rabbi Perr, Mrs. Perr came into the room and, leaning against the door with her arms full of laundry, said, "You know, it is a gift for us to have you here." How could such a confused, undirected shell of a Jew be a gift to her, I wondered? "It is a gift that you are sharing your journey with us," she went on. "My father would have been very happy to see you here." She smiled, and I knew that I could trust these people. So, that afternoon, as we sat together helping resolve other people's problems, I felt it was safe for me to express my own thoughts; and the Perrs' respect for others, as well as the lively curiosity that lived in them, made them want to hear me out.

But eventually the phone calls stopped, and I nudged the conversation around to the issue that was uppermost in my mind, the one I had been quietly struggling with—fear of God.

Rabbi Perr took a deep breath, then he sighed, and then he began his answer, though obliquely at first. "People," he said, "become gradually aware of and astonished at the worlds they don't know about that exist in their world. You suddenly become aware that there is such a thing as eternity, and you say, 'Well, I never knew there were things that were so critical and important.' "

Then he drew an analogy that surprised me. "It's the same as becoming aware that your wife is sensitive when you say something. You learn to be aware of that. And so, just like you develop *yiras-ishto,"*—fear of your wife—"you eventually develop *yiras ha-shamayim*"—fear of heaven.

I'd already discovered that even when his analogies seemed curious or unaccountable to me, they usually had their roots in scripture or tradition, and this one was no exception. One of the classical analogies for the fear of God urges us to fear God like a man who loves his wife and who is beloved by her. He isn't terrorized by her wrath, but rather is fearful of doing anything at all that might result in losing even a shred of the love he so treasures.

He was telling me, as I understood him, that the reality of a fearsome God is not at all apparent—no more than his example of eternity—but if I started by examining something similar that is close to hand—like another primary relationship, as with my wife—I would discover and become aware of the truth of this concept. But before I could be prepared to do that, I still needed to know *why* learning to fear God was so important. Rabbi Perr's response was unequivocal.

"I don't think you can separate ethics from belief in God and fear of retribution," he said, thoughtfully. "I don't think there is such a thing as ethics without fear of God." Then, with finality, he added, "I think that if a person is not a *yorei shamayim* [one who fears heaven], he is not going to be an ethical person."

That seemed a very hard view of human nature, but he went on to clarify his position by saying that this didn't mean we should equate fear of God with fear of punishment. "I've never heard Mussar people talk about hell and punishment," he said. "Never. When I hear that kind of talk I know automatically that those people don't have a Mussar tradition. They may think they're into Mussar because they've read something in books—and books are full of hell and punishment, no question about it."

His eyes flashed then as he took off down a cascading waterfall of ideas. "And, by the way, I don't think a person can go through life without a fear of hell. Because if you understand what goes on in this life, it's hard to believe that people should get away with it! But Mussar doesn't contain a lot of that, even in terms of unspoken reality. It is not presented that you are going to hell if you don't have good *middos*."

He was making an important distinction. There is indeed a concept of hell in Judaism that Mussar adopts, and, seeing how much evil people seem to get away with in this life, it is reassuring to envision them facing an ultimate reckoning. That idea might even help us to straighten out our own selves, to some extent. But this isn't really where a sensitive and contemporary Mussar teacher like Rabbi Perr wants us to put our emphasis. Instead, we are encouraged to work to improve our soul-traits because that's how we can fulfill our innate impulse to make something better of ourselves, to reach up toward our potential, which is to radiate holiness into this world, for the sake of ourselves and others.

And yet fear of God does show up most strikingly in the Mussar literature—just as Rabbi Perr said it did—as fear of divine punishment, and its corollary, anticipation of reward, if not in this life, then certainly in the next. The soul endures after death, and it is the soul that ultimately stands to receive judgment. The Bible and Talmud provide a picture of how the process goes. "When a man departs to his eternal home, all his deeds are enumerated before him and he is told: such and such a thing you have done, in such and such a place, on that day." The result, Ezekiel tells us, is that "the righteousness of the righteous shall be accounted to him alone, and the wickedness of the wicked shall be accounted to him alone."

But Rabbi Perr provided me with a view of heavenly punishment I'd never heard before, although it was one that fit perfectly with the Mussar way of thinking. "I have to tell you what I've heard from the Mussar masters," he said. "They say that you are going to come to the next world and they are going to show you what you *could* have been. They are going to show you the guy who was the same as you, and what he made of himself. And you are going to stand there and you are going to look at him for a million years! And that's just the beginning. Because you lost your opportunity."

Other traditional descriptions of heavenly reward and punishment, I have to confess, read to me like an ethnographic account of strange penal customs from some bizarre far-off land. And yet this one was far more frightening. No hellfires, no piercing, just an eternity wracked with regret for the opportunities you missed in this life, for squandering the chance you were handed to seek purity and perfection.

Fear of God can work for us, Mussar tells us, by helping us to grasp those chances that are given to us here on earth and so avoid an eternity of heavenly regrets. Holding that thought in mind can help us to stick to the commitments and resolutions we might make as part of our efforts to cultivate awareness, alter the levels of our soul-traits, and resist the blandishments of the devilish *yetzer ha-ra*. It will work for us, in effect, as a motivator. It was Mrs. Perr who made this quite clear to me when she said, "What's going to keep you to this discipline? It requires a calling that is bigger than you, that is going to discipline you to do this.

Just being a disciplined person, that's not enough. That's not going to make you a *ba'al Mussar*"—a Mussar master.

But even though I could see how divine retribution might work as a heavenly carrot and stick to keep us moving forward on our path toward self-perfection, I still couldn't seem to get my modern mind to designate fear a desirable mind-state and a spiritual goal. While there is plenty in the Mussar literature that says just that—that we should cultivate an attitude of cowering and shuddering at our own inadequacy, in the face of a judging God—I was very relieved when I discovered that Mussar also teaches us that there is a way to understand "fear" not as a state of constant anxiety or craven terror, but rather as something much more uplifting.

I found one of the most wonderful and surprising analogies for a positive understanding of *yirat ha-shamayim*, the fear of heaven, in an obscure Mussar book called *In the Footsteps of Yirah*. "To what may *yirah* be likened?" it asks. "To the tremor of fear that a father feels when his beloved young son rides on his shoulders as he dances with him and rejoices before him, taking care that he not fall off. Here there is joy that is incomparable, pleasure that is incomparable. And the fear tied up with them is pleasant too . . . It is clear to the father that his son is riding securely upon him and will not fall back, for he constantly remembers him, not for a moment does he forget him. His son's every movement, even the smallest, he feels, and he ensures that his son will not sway from his place, nor incline sideways—his heart is, therefore, sure, and he dances and rejoices."

Then the writer translates this analogy into spiritual terms that apply to our own lives. "If a person is sure that the 'bundle of his life's meaning' is safely held high by the shoulders of his awareness, he knows that this bundle will not fall backwards, he will not forget it for a moment, he will remember it constantly, with *yirah* he will keep it safe."

Who is the father? Awareness. Who is the son? The meaning in our lives. So, mature awareness supports the value in our lives. And where does fear figure in? As the positive sensation we foster to heighten our awareness. It keeps us awake, and so helps us take care of the meaning in our lives.

Here was a positive, thrilling, and uplifting facet of fear to which I could relate much more readily than tremulous weeping. And as I went deeper into Mussar, I discovered that the teachers in the tradition identify an even more exalted dimension to what we commonly label "fear." Rabbi Israel Salanter and others direct our attention to the feeling of overwhelming awe that comes over us when we perceive divine majesty in the world. Awe is that momentous—and sometimes terrifying—sensation that arises when we are pierced by the perception of our own tiny form teetering precariously on the lip of a vast, unfathomable universe that came into existence through no act of ours, and that carries us hurtling through space toward a destiny we can't even imagine.

When I translate this into terms of my own experience, it's the feeling I've had standing at the very edge of a majestic vista, such as the Grand Canyon, or when I've allowed my mind to go as far as it can to grasp the vastness of space, or when I've stopped to examine the perfect natural symmetry of a spiraling sea shell. It's something I feel in my belly, a little like vertigo, but exalted. I feel small but whole. The universe is a vast and detailed gyring domain, and I'm part of it—tiny but belonging. At those moments, life seems to me incredible.

One of my most vivid childhood memories is of pulling back the curtain on a sleepy winter's morning to discover a stark whiteness spread over trees, roads, and houses as far as my sleepy eyes could see. Overnight, the city suburb had been transformed into a silent frosted wonderland. Pewter gray skies poured out big, fat snowflakes that drifted down to powder every surface. Later, out shoveling the driveway or playing hockey in the street, we would sometimes stop to examine the finely filigreed flakes that clung lightly to a dark sleeve or the back of a glove. It impressed us then that a snowflake endures only for a second, before melting away at the faintest breath. Sometimes we would let them fall on our bare hands and watch, savoring the fleeting, precarious instant when the small, intricate lacy structure held tenaciously to its form. Suddenly it would give way and, in a twinkling, disappear into a tiny spot of dampness.

We could see, too, with the precise eyes of childhood, that all snowflakes are similarly shaped—a six-sided plate, discernible even amidst the feathered tracery of its delicately branching arms—yet no two were very much alike. How could there be such endless variation on a simple, common form?

I knew awe then. I touch it again when I open to it, giving myself over to contemplating one of nature's miracles. Awe like this comes up unbidden in unguarded moments, but because the Mussar masters recognized that the very experience of awe has a directly transformative impact, working deep change in the architecture of our hearts, they tell us that it's also something we ought to cultivate. We do that by slowing down and opening ourselves up to perceiving the many wonders of the world around us, great and small, through which we can detect the majesty that lies beneath their surface.

And so Mussar acknowledges that our experience of awe can come with equal measures of exaltation and terror, and that's the reason the word *yirah* means both fear and awe. Once I had grasped that duality, the concept became much more palatable for me, and I began to get an inkling of the spiritual possibilities it contained.

Having come to this appreciation that fear of God can validly mean terror of heavenly retribution, but equally can lead us to seek out the awesomeness of divine majesty in this world, I was again reminded by Rabbi Perr that this understanding would serve me only if I put it into play in my daily life. Because, as always, Mussar teachings are grounded in the here and now. "We only have here," he said. "The Alter of Novarodock says that this world is more important than the next world. Forget about the next world, he says in one place. Forget about the next world! This world is more important than anything else. One minute in this world doing the right thing is more important than the whole next world."

But even doing the right thing is not enough. Equally important—if not more so—is doing it for the right reasons and in the right way. Rabbi Perr talked to me about the heavy responsibility involved in making decisions. He said he needed to believe in an ultimate reckoning in order to take his duty seriously. The way he saw it, he would be held accountable not only for being right or wrong but also for how careful and thoughtful or sloppy he had been. As we were walking back to the yeshiva for evening prayers that day, he interpreted a teaching just to make this point: what motivates us to move to action may be even more important than the ends we seek.

First he quoted me a saying: "Do not be like those servants who serve their master to receive a portion, but rather be as those servants who serve their masters not to receive a portion. And let the fear of heaven be upon you."

Then he went right on to explain. "Let's say the master has received information that there is going to be a heavy rain, and his grain is still out in the field. His year's harvest will be destroyed. He calls together all his slaves, and what does he say? He says, 'Men, gotta go out and bring it in.'

"How does he make the slaves work? A foolish master would beat them with a stick, but if he beats them with a stick, he will soon discover that he gets less done. So instead he says, 'Whoever brings in the most wheat today is going to come with me to the King David Deli tonight and order the most expensive item on the menu, at my pleasure. We'll have a bottle of wine and a nice supper together.'

"So what happens? The slaves all get to work. Finally, at the end of the day the master asks the foreman who brought in the most wheat, and he says, 'Jimmy. Jimmy brought in twenty-five bushels.'

"So the master says, 'Okay, Jimmy, what are you going to order? Steak? Let me hear what you're going to have.'

"And Jimmy says, 'Boss, I didn't bring in those twenty-five bushels for that. I brought them in for *you*. How could I let the rain destroy your grain?' "

Rabbi Perr walked along, shaking his head. "He gave up that meal," he concluded, "but he got the boss. That night, as the boss

126

was lying in bed, he started to think, 'Maybe Jimmy is cold. Maybe he needs another blanket.' So he takes the extra blanket off his bed and goes to where the servants are sleeping, and he says, 'Hey, Jimmy, I thought you might be cold. I also brought you an extra pillow. Hey, Jimmy, maybe you should come move into the house with me.'

"So Jimmy understood what happens if you 'don't serve the master to receive a meal, but serve the master *not* to receive a meal.' "

We walked a few more paces in silence, and then he stopped, and he turned to me, asking, "How do we understand our relationship to God? By understanding how human beings work. Imagine what it means to God for you to serve Him not to receive anything?"

We resumed walking, and he returned to the final phrase of the saying he had originally quoted to me. "And the saying added the words 'let the fear of heaven be upon you' because a master you can fool but God you can't. You can't just get up and say"—and now he cupped his hand to his mouth and called upward in a singsong voice—" 'O God, I'm serving you for Your sake.' " Then he added quietly, " 'So now do me.' You have to remember to fear God so it will be genuine."

He shook his head. "That's an unbelievable teaching. Wouldn't you say it's an unbelievable teaching of how to get into God's grace?"

But, I wondered aloud, was that really the motive behind the teaching?

"Yes," he answered quietly. "I think it's telling us how to win God, how to get God on our side."

And then he explained why this sort of teaching is so necessary and helpful for us. "There are tests of a person, and without fear a person doesn't withstand the tests, because he's ready to throw it all away. Why? Because we're built that way, because our job in life is to grow. And to grow we have to make choices. And to make our choices real, we have to realize that we can fall." Believing that our choices have real consequences can give us strength to face life's tests. Then we are much more likely to come through victorious, and instead of being crushed, we grow.

We were just climbing the steps to the door of the yeshiva when he said something that really amazed me, and that drove home for me the humanity that lies at the heart of his teaching, and his own humanity too. Rabbi and Mrs. Perr still live in the house where they raised six children. Those children are now grown and on their own, and only Mrs. Perr's elderly and infirm mother now lives with them. "If it were not for the fear of heaven," Rabbi Perr said, "I don't think I would have the ethical conviction to keep my mother-in-law in the house. It is such a strain on my wife and on our relationship that it would be so easy to rationalize sending her to a nursing home. Even the difference would be small to her. But when I remember the final accounting, it strengthens my commitment."

OPENING THE GATE

CONTEMPLATION ON AWE
AND THE GRANDEUR OF GOD

So *yirah* can mean "fear," and it can also mean "awe." Which of these meanings you relate to is mostly a matter of your needs and disposition, and especially of how you want or need to work with the concept. The variety wrapped up in this one notion illustrates how Mussar provides us with choices that take into account the differences between people, and the differing needs people have at different stages of the journey. Different tools for different jobs, we can say, all there for us to choose among as we go about our tasks of working on and for the soul.

While I now understand and appreciate more fully how our aptitude for fear can be put to work in a positive way on the spiritual path, in truth I personally still find myself more drawn to working with the experience of awe.

Rabbi Moshe Chaim Luzzatto has said that awe can be achieved only through "the contemplation of the Grandeur of God." This kind of contemplation is accessible and practical for all of us to undertake just by looking at the wondrous creations that surround us. But the Mussar teachers help guide us toward the experience of awe that is the most profound aspect of *yirat ha-shamayim* by giving us contemplations that will walk our minds through levels of appreciation until—as we open to it— boundless awe settles on us.

Ibn Pakuda gives us several such guided contemplations. In one place, he suggests that we contemplate the majesty and wonder of a natural process that occurs within us several times every day, but that we hardly ever stop to consider—digestion. He leads us step by step through all the stages that food passes through from the moment it first enters our lips, which have the job of closing the mouth, through the tasks of teeth and tongue, to the miracle of the rhythmic dance of peristalsis, and so on, until all that is good in the food is extracted and circulated throughout the body, while the waste is separated out and disposed of. He causes us to pay attention and be amazed, and, ultimately, to perceive the awe that digestion—and all "natural" processes—truly warrants.

The Mussar teachers developed and appreciated guided contemplations because they understood that imagery held vividly in the mind imprints itself directly to the heart, bypassing the intellect. They recognized that we can harness the power of imagination and thought to help us on our spiritual journeying.

I personally like to follow a guided contemplation on the vastness of space—awe of the macrocosm; and, at the other end of the spectrum, I have used a guided contemplation on snowflakes, which I love. The next time you see one of those miraculous, tiny, unique, six-sided wonders, pause and consider how lightly it has come into the world, and how in a breath it is gone. To do this is to understand profoundly the opening words from William Blake's *Auguries of Innocence:* "To find a world in a grain of sand / And a heaven in a wild flower / Hold infinity in the palm of your hand / And eternity in an hour."

Rabbi Eliyahu Dessler has left us a contemplation meant to foster awe that we can follow exactly, with no need for any modern elaboration or revision. In it, he explores the notion of eternity and leads us, step by step, into a state of boundless wonderment. As you follow the contemplation, your job is to let go of the analytical mind and open yourself to experiencing the awe that arises from these images of the vastness of time:

Imagine an enormous mountain of sand situated next to the sea. Every thousand years a great bird wings its way to the top of the mountain, takes one grain of sand in its beak and drops it into the sea. Another thousand years must go by until the next grain is removed. The exercise is to attempt to visualize, or experience in imagination, the lapse of a thousand years . . . One begins by imagining the events of one day, then two days, a week, a month, two months, a year, etc., recapitulating each time, as far as possible, the temporal "feel" of a day or a week, and resisting the temptation to lapse into conceptualization by saying "and so on" or "as we said before." When one has "felt" a year in this manner, one multiplies this progressively until one reaches a lifetime, a century, two centuries, three centuries . . . until one arrives at a thousand years. Then—the bird comes and takes another grain of sand from the mound. But the whole mound is still there! One has to start the whole process over again for the third grain, and for the fourth, and so on and so on . . . And even when that unimaginably distant moment is reached and the last grain of sand disappears into the ocean—eternity has still hardly begun!

If one allocates, say, ten minutes a day to this mental exercise, the empty words "eternal life" will soon have acquired a "felt" meaning which they certainly did not have before.

CHAPTER SEVEN

THE GATE OF
TRUST IN GOD

"A person who tries to practice bitahon *while leaving himself a backup plan is like a person who tries to learn how to swim but insists on keeping one foot on the ground."*

—RABBI YOSEF YOZEL HURVITZ,

THE ALTER OF NOVARODOCK

ear of God, even if it's experienced as awe, can leave us trembling, but Mussar doesn't abandon us to that fate. Instead it provides another guideline to help us find comfort and confidence in this world, frightening though it might be.

Mussar urges us to put our trust in God—that same God whom we've been told to fear—and tells us that this trust is so important it is to be considered a soul-trait in and of itself. That quality is called, in Hebrew, *bitahon*. Those who have it in abundance move through life with confidence and courage, while the curse of those with too little is constant worry and fear.

When Mrs. Perr's father, Rabbi Nekritz, was in Siberia at the beginning of World War II, locals would ask him why he and his family had been sent into exile. "To teach you *bitahon*," he would answer with a smile. And all the time he was there, he never bent, was never crushed. When he arrived in Brooklyn after the war, he was neither broken nor bitter.

Rabbi Nekritz had a formidable teacher of *bitahon* of his own in the Alter of Novarodock, Rabbi Yosef Yozel Hurvitz, who considered this soul-trait so important that in his later years he would sign his letters only "B.B.," meaning *ba'al* [master] of *bitahon*. He so encouraged the practice of trust that, during the 1917 revolution in Russia, he urged his students to brave the conflict and chaos to continue their studies and to propagate Torah and Mussar. The fearlessness that he instilled in them was so great that, in their zeal to preach spiritual renewal, they are reported to have seized the lectern during Communist rallies, argued with court prosecutors, and broken into Mussar chants in the middle of proceedings.

The question of how we might be able to develop even a shadow of this kind of fearless trust in our own lives, and what it can do for the soul, came up one morning while I was having breakfast with Rabbi Perr in his office.

It was after morning prayers, and the men and boys were standing around the study hall, wishing each other good morning while removing their *tefillin*, wrapping the straps around their boxes, and stowing them in their little cases, carefully folding their *tallises*, storing them into their embroidered velvet bags, and then sliding those bags into plastic covers. They buttoned their shirt cuffs and slipped on the jacket sleeves that had been thrown off to make way for the leather thong each had wrapped around his (usually left) arm in fulfillment of the biblical commandment: "You shall bind them for a sign upon your hand."

Then someone announced that he had brought a tray of dough-nuts for the boys, and the room quickly emptied. I was still lin-gering, as had become my habit, partly because I savored that sweet moment of lightness hovering between prayers and the start of the day, and partly because I wanted to be sure not to miss any unannounced teaching or ritual that might be about to occur. When Rabbi Perr came over and invited me for breakfast, I happily followed as he led the way toward his office, splitting the milling crowd like a black-hulled icebreaker, his tall hat its smokeless stack.

With a sigh, he lowered himself into his high-backed chair and I took my usual place on the other side of the desk, which was heaped with so many layers of papers, letters, and books that not the tiniest speck of its surface was visible. A young boy ma-terialized to take our breakfast order, and Rabbi Perr asked for his usual cold cereal and milk and then, nodding in my direction, he asked, "Bagel? With cream cheese? And orange juice?" My order had become something of a regular, too.

The boy left and the rabbi picked up a small piece of paper from atop one of the piles, looked at it, and sighed again.

"What is it?" I asked.

He answered without taking his eyes from the paper. "I had a new timer installed on the stove at home. It cost me two hun-dred and seventy-nine dollars and now I find out there's a prob-lem. When it turns on automatically on Shabbos, a buzzer goes off. I can't turn it off and I can't have this buzzer going all of Shabbos."

"There must be some way to disconnect the buzzer," I com-miserated.

"Yeah, disconnect the whole thing," he replied dejectedly.

Then he shook his head, threw down the paper, and swiveled his chair to face me more directly.

"So?" he said. *"Nu?"* This was his invitation to bring up anything I might have on my mind. Now his eyes smiled, and when they did the little wrinkles in their corners lifted upward and smiled too.

"I'm feeling a little more at ease during prayers," I informed him.

"You look completely laid back to me," he responded.

"Well, not quite."

"No one is going to do or say anything about anything, you know that, don't you?" he offered by way of comfort.

"I do, of course, but it isn't so rational."

"You know," he said, laying down a plank from which to launch into a story, "there's someone I've been very close to for many years, a smart guy, who had a fear of being called to the Torah for an *aliyah*."

Since an *aliyah*—being called to recite a short and routine blessing over the Torah scroll—is a common honor, I wondered how it could have caused Rabbi Perr's friend such anxiety.

"He was afraid to take an *aliyah*," the rabbi explained, "because he was afraid he wouldn't know how to make the blessing, and he didn't want to read the words from a prayer book because he was embarrassed. But he was petrified that he would make a mistake and people would laugh at him. To describe the extent of his fear, when his wife became pregnant he knew he would get an *aliyah* when the baby was born, and he called me up in total panic. He could hardly talk, and he was going to be sick over it for nine months."

At that point, the boy returned with our breakfast, setting the plates right on top of whatever lay in front of us on the desk. After washing hands and reciting a blessing, Rabbi Perr poured his cereal into a bowl, added some milk, and while I spread the cream cheese on my bagel, he went on with his story.

"So I told him just to prepare himself to be laughed at, to picture himself being laughed at. And so? After that he didn't have a problem with the whole thing."

Pausing with his spoon halfway to his mouth, he added, "Acceptance is the key."

He swallowed, and then asked, "And how does one achieve acceptance? Well, you can do that in a very secular way by saying, 'Look, I can't do anything about this, so I'm stuck, so I'm just going to go into it and hope for the best.' But there's also acceptance that has a religious underpinning.

"There is a saying that you don't have a penny more or a penny less than you're supposed to have in this world, and if you have a little bit too much, He's going to take it away by making you order a new timer for the stove that's absolutely not going to work for you. So He's going to take away two hundred and seventy-nine dollars because if you had been smart you would have given it to charity and you wouldn't have had it to pay for the timer. And the first one wouldn't have busted. You just didn't give enough."

He smiled. "Therefore you take it, and you laugh." He shrugged. "And you laugh," he repeated, his voice rising in an audible shrug. "The same thing goes for honor," he continued, dipping his spoon into his bowl once again.

Was he changing the subject? No, he was just zeroing in on the cause that lies a level below fear. If fear is the symptom, a concern for honor can be the cause.

"Every gift you have," he continued between spoonfuls of cereal, "whether it is material or emotional—such as people showing you honor—comes from heaven. You never get more or less from others than is precisely decreed for you. There are no tests, no obstacles, no shame that has not been decreed. One day you can walk into morning prayers without your shirt on and no one will notice. But another day, you can walk in wearing your finest suit and someone will spill a bowl of borscht on your jacket, and you'll be stuck with it for the rest of the day. That's been decreed, too. There's no way out of it. And accepting that sort of relieves you of the concern."

Stroking the corners of his mustache with his fingers, he added, "When you understand that you're not in control, you can't perfect yourself, and you can't protect yourself from what is decreed, that's *bitahon*—trust in God. In most things, *bitahon* can help."

The trust in God exhibited by the Mussar masters is legendary. They followed their commitments and accepted their fate fearlessly in the face of whatever life brought them. One of Rabbi Perr's favorite stories is about a Mussar student who was exiled to Siberia and whose attitude was so trusting and carefree that the camp authorities believed he was mad and so left him alone—which is just what he had expected to happen!

Those of us who have not developed this kind of trust tend to get a rough buffeting from life. Things happen, and we find ourselves swept up in waves of fear or worry—or, just as likely, pride or happiness. Either way, we're vulnerable to being lifted up or blasted down by whatever force happens to be swirling around us. And then, in an effort to overcome the fear or hold onto the happiness, we try to manipulate the situation to fit our own design. We flatter anyone we think can help us and use others to suit our purpose.

It's not very pretty, and the turbulence of emotions can be exhausting. It happens to me whenever I identify myself as the prime actor in my life, the master of my fate. When life blesses me with gifts, "I" have made a success of myself; when life is bleak, it's because "I" have failed.

A soul infused with trust in God, on the other hand, is graced with equanimity, stillness, and quiet, and is no longer at the mercy of these emotional firestorms. Having *bitahon* means you have a profound understanding that you didn't ask to be put here, you didn't write the script, and neither did the person who might be helping or hindering you at any given moment, so you might as well relax and trust. But that doesn't mean you now believe that only good things will happen to you. That isn't how life works. Trust in God isn't going to give you any kind of special edge—it won't help your team win the next game and it won't cure your cancer. When you strengthen the soul-trait that is *bitahon*, you gain equanimity, because you have set yourself up to accept whatever ultimately comes to pass. Your will is aligned with the larger Will, and so you are not going to be disturbed by the way things go, whether or not it is the way you had hoped. "The essence of trust," ibn Pakuda writes in *The Duties of the Heart*, "is the tranquility of the soul enjoyed by the one who trusts."

This might sound like a fatalistic attitude, but actually having this sort of trust still doesn't relieve us of our obligation to act. It doesn't mean we just sit back and wait to see what God has in store for us, because it is still important that we make an effort—and, in fact, in most instances effort is required, because the Jewish tradition prohibits reliance on miracles. It's a bit of a paradox, because everything is decreed from on high, and yet we still have free will and an obligation to act on our own behalf. The rabbis don't resolve this paradox, they just affirm the truth of both propositions. Rabbi Akiva puts it succinctly: "Everything is foreseen, yet freedom of choice is given."

In any case, Mussar is a very down-to-earth discipline, and it would run counter to our common sense if we were told not to put every one of our gifts and our energies to work in order to try to make things turn out the way we think will be best. But Mussar also warns us that we would be foolish—and arrogant—if we believed that by our actions alone we could control what happens in our lives, because in reality everything that comes to pass is the product of many elements, some of which are clearly beyond our command. Often we aren't even aware of all the factors involved. And if we can't know everything about our situation, there really isn't any point in getting all worked up over what the outcome might be. Rabbi Perr tells a wonderful story that drives home just this point.

There was once a Talmudic scholar who was so impoverished that he often had no money for food, and yet he refused to accept charity or gifts. So a group of students at the yeshiva in the town where he lived made it their project to come up with all kinds of subterfuges to help him and his family. For example, they would buy cans of tuna fish, then scuff and dent them before selling them to the scholar for a dollar a can, telling him that they had been salvaged from a train wreck.

One of these students took it upon himself to change burnt-out light bulbs anytime he went to visit the scholar. He would stash a new bulb in his pocket and, the moment the older man wasn't watching, he'd make the exchange. One day when the scholar stepped out of the room, the student hopped up on a chair and started to unscrew a dead bulb. But just while he was in mid-screw, the man returned.

"What are you doing?" he asked.

"Oh, just taking out this light bulb. I noticed it wasn't working," the young man replied.

"Just leave it," the scholar said. "I've noticed that when they're left alone for a while, they rest up and start to go again."

There were factors at work he simply couldn't see.

But even though we can't determine what will happen to us, because we can never know or control *all* the factors, we still need to act on those elements that seem to be in our power, and then, as we face the outcome, we can rely upon our cultivated trust in God.

As the Mussar tradition teaches it, trust in God is not the same thing as faith. Faith is more of a global concept, involving a belief in the existence of God; trust is much more personal, and concerns the relationship between God and oneself. A great twentieth-century Talmudist, the Chazon Ish, has written that "faith and trust are a single entity, except that faith involves the general worldview of a person while trust involves his perspective on himself. Faith is theoretical while trust is practical," indicating once more Mussar's concern with the inner life of the soul as it lives in this world.

When our *bitahon* is weak, we lack trust, and this shows up in our lives as worry. The Chazon Ish tells us that "worrying is the greatest sin of all," because it is impossible to worry and have trust at the same time, and it is a sin not to trust in God. Worry is the fear that things will not turn out as *we* want them to; developing trust allows us to believe that they will turn out exactly as *they* should, and is, therefore, a powerful antidote to worry and fear.

When I suggested to Rabbi Perr that leading a life of trust, free from worry, balanced and calm, seemed an unattainable ideal, he was quick to reassure me. "If you're in the subject," he said, "it's something doable, and if you're not, it looks impossible, like a lot of things."

It's a topic he touches on often in his *shmoozes,* as he did that day when I, and fifteen or so yeshiva students, gathered around him in the study hall. The rabbi opened his book and read to himself before beginning to speak quietly, his eyes still on the book before him.

"Most of the fears that grip our minds amount to nothing," he began. "Nothing, really. We worry just because we lack for trust in God. Through learning and practice we can bring out that trust. Good, strong *bitahon* changes a person's life totally, from the inside out."

He then went on to describe the scattered condition of most people's souls. If the goal of Mussar is to teach us how to develop inner wholeness—or holiness—then a scattered soul is the exact opposite of what we seek. The concentration of the soul is the condition of its genius, out of which arises vibrant wisdom. "There is no happiness in a scattered soul," Rabbi Perr continued. "There is *mishigas* [craziness] and there is worry, but there is no peace, no calmness of soul." And calmness of soul is the barometer by which we measure trust.

To illustrate the power of *bitahon,* Rabbi Perr drew on the story of the Exodus. "Remember," he said forcefully, driving home the words, "that for forty years—and this was baked into our bones—for forty years we ate *manna* in the desert, for forty years a whole nation did not have what to eat and depended on the loving-kindness that dropped food to them from heaven. For forty years, every single day."

He took a deep breath then, and continued, only more quietly. "They lived in the desert with the purest *bitahon*. If someone even tried to save food from one day to the next, it would rot. They had to trust that food would come. And they were provided for!

"We have been taught that a righteous person is one who eats for today and is satisfied."

Then he translated the lesson for his contemporary audience. "You know, in my parents' generation, they saved everything and anything, because who knew if one day they would need it, or it could be put to use somehow."

I knew what he meant. My father, until the day he died, saved nails. Even the rustiest, most bent, thrice-used nail had a place in one of his glass jars. Since he died, no one has had the heart to throw them away.

"Why did they economize? Because they were afraid. Did it make them happy? Not one day. Only those who live with trust and snuggle under the shadow of God have the blessing of happiness."

Having uttered this truth, he paused briefly to sketch a more lighthearted illustration. "Just like a kid comes along and says to his parents, 'I'm afraid of this, and I'm afraid of that,' and they say, 'You don't have to worry about that. We take care of that for you.' So the kid says, 'What happens if I get sick?' 'We have medical insurance.' 'And what about . . .' 'We take care of that for you.'

"And without *bitahon,*" he peered darkly from under his eyebrows, "worry and worry and worry. Worry doesn't cost money; it doesn't require a degree. You don't have to take courses for it or get a license for it. In fact, it's open to amateurs. You don't even have to be an expert in how to worry."

There was a ripple of laughter then among the students, but it stopped quickly enough when Rabbi Perr sighed long and deep and proclaimed, "There *are* experts in worry, let me tell you. What will be, and what will be, and what will be? They get up in the morning and they don't enjoy one day of their lives. And what is that?" He flattened his hands on the table before him. "That is not a life.

"A person has to acquire the knowledge that he's not the one doing it. Simple as that. He has to know who is running the world. Not that he should not make certain efforts, but if something is not good for him in one way, he will see it'll be good for him in another way. That's the bottom line on *bitahon.*"

And that was the bottom line on Rabbi Perr's *shmooze.* Afterward, when I sat with him in his office, he peered at me intently and then asked, "They can't possibly understand everything I'm saying to them, but you understood it, didn't you?"

I said I thought I'd understood, but that wasn't enough for him. He asked me again, and this time I assured him unequivocally that I had. Because, in fact, I did. I'd spent fifteen years of my adult life immersed in the world of business with the conscious intention of making enough money so that I could securely re-engage the spiritual side of my nature, which I had mostly put aside by then. I'd been unable to see how I could survive with spirituality as the primary focus of my life, and there had seemed no other way for me to protect my spiritual goals but to take care of the material first, after which I'd be free to delve into the life of the spirit. Ha! I might have been a filmmaker, but I'd needed a sharp poke in the eye to make me see that I was not the one writing the script for my life.

My plan had been built on lack of trust. I'd been living as one of those untrusting souls whom ibn Pakuda describes as taking out collateral on God, in case He didn't come through with the payments I seemed to think I was owed. And in the end even that didn't work out. Despite polished mission statements and long-term goals, I still found myself ultimately having to live in a way that called on me to find the trust in my heart. And I couldn't help wondering where I might be today if I'd started living that way thirty years ago.

When I told all this to Rabbi Perr, he stroked his beard as he listened, and then he provided me with one last cautionary tale to take home with me that day. It was in the form of a parable he attributed to the Vilna Gaon, the eighteenth-century inspiration of contemporary Orthodox Judaism.

"A king once had a ladder put against a wall, and he said that whoever mounted the ladder to the top would get his daughter in marriage. Of course, all the soldiers were vying to be the first to run up the ladder. The first one was two-thirds up, and when he hit the next step it just opened up and he fell through. The step snapped closed again, and now the rest of them weren't running quite so fast.

"The second one went up a little more hesitantly, and as he

stepped gingerly on that step the same thing happened. It opened up, he fell through, and then it snapped shut again.

"Now no one wanted to try, until finally a fellow came along who ran very quickly up the ladder with a lot of power, and when he came to that step, he jumped with all his might to the rung above it, and he landed safely. It didn't open up. And he received the daughter in marriage."

Rabbi Perr took off his glasses and set them on his desk. "This parable tells us that although the King has made a trick step, He is seeking the one who trusts him enough to know that He's not just out to break everybody's leg. He's the one the King wants for a son-in-law. Of course, it's a tricky thing to do—"

"The next rung could have been booby-trapped, too," I suggested.

"Yeah," Rabbi Perr quickly responded, "but not likely. The one who jumped, he figured out that the next step was going to be solid. How did he know that? Because he trusted that, in the end, the King didn't want to break everybody's neck. Many might fall, but the trick rung was there only to reveal who was going to be the one who would conquer."

A long silence hung between us then, filled by the hum from the next-door study hall buzzing through the wall.

"I could not manage without it," he said finally, meaning trust in God. "I could not manage without it. All my life has been, I would say, miraculous. I could not manage without it. His kindness to me, and His teaching me, and His showing me. If you take one step in His direction, He comes to seek you too. He searches you out. He may not speak to you, but you will find that He is there. You'll see it. He's there with you. He will guide you. And I am sure that it will happen to you. There's no question."

"It's already happening," I replied. "It's happening at this moment, now."

OPENING THE GATE

EXERCISES TO DO IN THE WORLD TO PRACTICE AND IMPROVE *MIDDOT* (SOUL-TRAITS)

That Friday evening, I was a guest for dinner at Rabbi and Mrs. Perr's home. The day's activities had faded with the light, and Rabbi Perr sat at the head of the table, resplendent in a long, dark-blue satin coat he wore only on the Sabbath. We had eaten our fill and were deep into the kind of free-floating conversation that comes when there is time to spare and ideas just seem to flow from one to another.

Suddenly there was a knock at the door and, without waiting for an answer, a middle-aged couple entered the house to be met with a warm and familiar greeting.

Mrs. Perr introduced the visitors, Moishe and Lynn Broide, and explained to them my interest in Mussar, which had brought me to Far Rockaway. Only later did I discover that Moishe Broide's own Mussar pedigree included his mother's grandfather, who was the Alter of Slobodka, and his father's grandfather, who was the brother of the Alter of Kelm.

Later that evening, as the conversation ambled along, Moishe leaned over to me without overture and said quietly, "Studying Mussar is nothing. You must *do* Mussar."

Having overheard his friend, Rabbi Perr immediately added, "That came from Mussar, because Mussar is that way. Because it's not just books." To the contrary, Mussar encourages people to practice and improve their *middot,* or soul-traits, in the school of real life.

It was with just that in mind that some Mussar teachers—especially in the Novarodock tradition—gave their students exercises to be conducted out in the world that would help to develop or improve their soul-traits. These tests were real and the learning was immediate. If, for example, the student's task was to "uproot love of honor," he would be told to go into a hardware store and ask for bread, and then to a drug store to ask for nails. The student making these absurd requests would soon find himself on the receiving end of people's scorn, which was, of course, one of the goals of the exercise. Not only would he quickly come to see how deluded is the quest for self-honor, but he would also be freed from the clutches of pride. And, finally, the exercise would provide good practice for retaining inner equanimity and God-focus in the midst of surrounding distraction.

As an exercise to develop their *bitahon,* students would be given a one-way train ticket to a destination two hundred kilometers from the yeshiva and sent out with not a coin in their pockets. They would be told to make their way directly back to the yeshiva, and they were not allowed to ask anyone for help. They had no one but God in whom to trust.

There isn't a single soul-trait that can't be altered in this way, by exercises undertaken in our daily life. Reading about it in books, understanding what *should* be, is not the same as actually doing it. It's the difference between theory and practice.

Elaborating on this theme, Rabbi Perr told me about a Mussar group he had run for young people. "We had about twenty people in the group, professionals and various others, and we used to meet once a week, performing various Mussar exercises. Once we worked for a period of time on overcoming shyness or awkwardness. We undertook various things, and each member of the group volunteered in his own way to do something he knew would not be easy for him, because it is very important.

"The purpose of the exercises is to show us that we don't need to be afraid of life. We can lean into it. When life throws us a test, we can lean into it. Just lean into it."

Then, having made his general point, he told me a story.

"Here in town, there's a *moyel*"—the person who performs ritual circumcisions—"who told me the story of his first experience. He'd been taught by another *moyel* using the finger of a rubber glove—how to fold it over, pull it, how to put the clamp on, how to put the shield on, how to cut it. So he practiced and practiced with the glove, and he had it all worked out.

"Then he came to his first *bris* [circumcision], and he made his cut and it started bleeding! Until then he'd only been cutting rubber gloves! So he started screaming, 'It's bleeding! *Gevalt*, it's bleeding!' Fortunately there was a doctor there who took over."

Rabbi Perr then broke into gales of laughter. "Theory and practice," he gasped. "Theory and practice."

Setting ourselves tasks that can be undertaken in the context of our everyday interactions is a powerful way to develop all our soul-traits, including trust in God. And since worry is the opposite of trust, it can give us some good material to use in our practice. We each have our own worries—yours will likely be different from mine—but it isn't the nature or content of the worry that matters so much as becoming conscious of when it is present, and naming it. "A-ha. There is worry." Because only with that awareness can we meet the worry with a counterbalancing practice.

We learn this from ibn Pakuda, who focuses his discussion of *bitahon* on the worrisome issue of livelihood, and advises us to use our means of making a living as a vehicle for practicing trust in God. One way of doing that would be to cultivate a wholehearted gratitude for the work we have. Rather than grasping after something else, we are told to look for, enumerate, and praise the good qualities in whatever work we are doing.

That doesn't mean, of course, that we will never have to make a change or confront superiors. But in those circumstances, too, we can challenge ourselves to go forward with an attitude of fearless trust.

We wouldn't want to try it without having cut a few rubber gloves first—that's the equivalent of Mussar's contemplation, meditation, and reflection—but at some point we need to graduate to the world of flesh and blood. The key to this practice is to shift our focus from trying to influence outcomes to developing the inner qualities we seek. When our actions are dedicated to developing our soul-traits, there is nothing to worry or fear, because we have trust, which leads us to accept whatever may result from those actions. By doing this, we transform our everyday deeds into exercises, and we refocus our efforts from trying to govern the course of our lives to trying to govern ourselves.

CHAPTER EIGHT

THE GATE OF WORKING IN THE WORLD

*"The foundation of the state of perfection is in matters
that are between a man and his neighbor."*
—RABBI ISRAEL SALANTER,
IMREI BINAH

One thing I noticed right away when I encountered Mussar was that it was a spiritual path that designated as life's goal something as elevated as anything I could imagine—becoming holy—but whose means were insistently rooted in everyday life. I realized then that this was a spiritual but not a mystical path, and Rabbi Perr confirmed that to me one day when he said, "When I was younger, I was much more attracted to the esoteric, but as I get older, I find that there is a great depth and beauty and meaning to simple things. I'm not so interested in the mystical. For me, there is enough mystery here in this reality." He paused, then added quietly, "There is enough mystery in this present moment." Redirecting attention to the here and now like that brought a moment of pure stillness into the room.

As my studies continued, however, it sometimes seemed to me that the Mussar teachers were so focused on the task of improving one's own soul that they paid scant attention to anything that might be called social action. This was certainly true in the world of the yeshiva, where the focus falls almost exclusively on studying the Talmud and Torah—although within the perspective of the yeshiva world, that *is* seen to be a form of social action, since study provides the blueprint for right living. But still, I wondered how a discipline so firmly dedicated to good deeds and ethics as is Mussar could advocate personal self-improvement and yet not be equally insistent that we become involved with the welfare of others.

When I voiced this concern to Rabbi Perr during one of our afternoon sessions in his office, he jumped to set me straight.

"There isn't one school of Mussar that believes a person should lead an isolated life," he began, his dark eyes focused directly on mine. "Although they all believe in having periods of self-contemplation, nobody believes in being isolated, unless they find themselves in a world that is so totally corrupt there is no way of escaping its influences or of attacking it. Then, they would believe in isolating themselves, because otherwise it would be too overwhelming for an individual to cope.

"But in any case," he continued thoughtfully, "there is no reason for isolation in today's world. There may be mistakes and innocence among people who are not pursuing the right way, but we are very fortunate because, in general, there is very little deep corruption in the Western world. Fundamentally it's a good world. Most people you can reach, and you can inform; you can make them better, and it is certainly our responsibility to try to make the world a better place."

That answer offered some reassurance, though it didn't quite satisfy my sense that somewhere in Mussar there might be more of an understanding of the quid pro quo between the work we do to improve ourselves and the work we engage in to improve the world, and of the fact that neither one can be neglected for the sake of the other.

"Sometimes," Rabbi Perr cautioned me, having taken off his glasses, which he was now waving in one hand, "people use reaching out as a substitute for reaching in. In our times, there is so much outward need that there is hardly any time for the internal contemplative life. You have to be careful not to let outer involvements distract you so you have no time for yourself. The Mussar teachers all taught that a person has to set aside time for himself. Hillel said it in the Talmud: 'If I am not for myself, who will be for me, and if I am only for myself, what am I?' But, on the other hand, it is possible to be too self-absorbed, and being active in the world can help you with that. There is that balance. A person is both a social creature and a lonely creature, and he has to find ways of serving both."

Assuming good intentions, he went on, "Reaching out is so, so important. Very often, when a person reaches out, he hears himself far better than if he were speaking only to himself. By teaching, for example, one begins to appreciate what one is teaching, and so, too, by representing something one grows in appreciation of what it is he represents. This can be a very useful tool for self-perfection, if the person has a lot of honesty and is soul-searching and does not want to be hypocritical. I think that many times that is even the best tool."

It seemed to me that he was returning to a subject we'd discussed before, the need not only to study Mussar but to *do* it. In that light, engagement in the world can be seen as a tool for bringing about inner change, although we have to recognize that the roots of our values, behaviors, and habits lie so deep within us that it still requires introspective work to ensure that change penetrates deeply enough to uproot and rework them. The methods and practices designed by the Mussar masters to be performed quietly upon ourselves complement our efforts in the world and make sure that they are genuine.

The Mussar teachers define three relationships that form the nexus of all spiritual work. Certain deeds are meant to be performed between a person and himself (this is called *bein adam l'atsmo*), others are to be between a person and God (*bein adam le-Makom*), and still others between a person and his neighbor, or his fellow human beings (*bein adam l'havero*). And we must be attentive to all three if we are to improve and perfect our own soul-traits.

Once more, Mussar calls on us to look at every experience in our lives as an opportunity to take a step toward perfecting the heart and allowing our holiness to shine through. In that context, the world at large is nothing less than a crucible in which to temper and balance our soul-traits, and in this way serving our community offers a prime opportunity for self-improvement. But the world is turned into a spiritual laboratory only when social action is understood not just as a matter of doing work *for* others, but also as an opportunity to do work *on* ourselves. When we reach out, it should be not simply because others are in need but also because we want at the same time to reach in, to enliven some trait within ourselves. Our acts are meant to help others and at the same time also to enhance our own characteristic of generosity, or to mute our pride, or to counter a tendency toward anger, or to mold some other trait we know needs work in us.

One story Rabbi Perr told me about Rabbi Israel Salanter makes this symbiosis very clear. "In 1850, there was a cholera epidemic in Lithuania that claimed many lives. He did what you'd expect of a community leader, encouraging people to stay calm and help out and so on, but that wasn't where it stopped for him. He jumped in to head up the relief activities. He took seventy of his students, and organized them to take care of sick people—these were strangers, not his own people. Remember, this was a terribly infectious disease, and he and his students were taking grave risks with their own health. Why did they do this? He said it himself, it was to learn to overcome fear, though not foolishly. He insisted that everyone follow the instructions of the physicians, and that every effort had to be made to preserve life, and once all that had been done, they were to trust in God. Those were the inner attitudes he wanted them to develop, and here was a very good testing ground."

Then Rabbi Perr zeroed in on the spiritual component that gives our work in the world its deepest value. "God wants your heart," he said. "Your check doesn't hurt either, but writing checks can be a way of just brushing off inner guilt and satisfying the need to participate. But He wants your heart. If a needy person walks in off the street, you can do something because you want to help that person, or you might want to look like you're helping someone, or you might want a reputation for helping people. There's a very big difference, and you're a totally different person if you do it one way or the other way. And it's all dependent on the inside, what's inside your head and heart."

In practice, this means that, as we extend ourselves to give to or help others, we divert our eyes to look within. There will be qualities of the heart—kindness, generosity, compassion—that we seek to manifest through our action, and so our inner eye trolls for any hint of mixed motives that might taint or defile the purity of the quality we seek to incarnate. Are we helping selflessly? Can we detect traces of desire for thanks and recognition? Is our response the result of our having entered compassionately into another person's pain? Or are we milking our giving to feed our sense of how superior we are? Do we perceive the needy person before us as a form of the divine image, or is a needy person *all* we see?

The Yiddish writer I. L. Peretz was not a Mussarist, but he wrote a story that goes to the heart of the Mussar way of helping out in the world. It takes place in the village of Nemirov in Eastern Europe, an undistinguished place much like so many other places Jews once called home. Every Friday during the month of Elul—the last chance for prayer and repentance before the Days of Awe, when every person's fate is sealed for the year to come—the rabbi of this village would vanish. He had ascended to heaven, the people told one another, where he was no doubt asking God to bring peace and goodness for the coming year.

It happened that a stranger came to the village during one holy season, and having heard about the rabbi's annual disappearances, decided that he would get to the heart of the mystery. So, one Thursday night, he sneaked into the rabbi's home, hid himself beneath the bed, and waited. Just before dawn, the rabbi arose and dressed himself not in the dignified frock coat and clean black hat that would be appropriate for his position, but in work pants, high boots, a thick hat, rough coat, and wide belt. He stuffed a rope in his pocket, tucked an ax in his belt, and left the house, followed by the villager.

The rabbi walked through the dark streets into the small forest that stood at the edge of the town. The man who was trailing him nearly fell to the ground in amazement when he saw the rabbi take up his ax and proceed to chop down one small tree after another, split them into logs, chop the logs into shorter lengths, and bundle them up with the rope. Then he slung the bundle over his shoulder and, with the villager still on his trail, proceeded to a small broken-down shack, where he knocked on the window.

"Who's there," asked the frightened, ailing woman inside.

"I, Vassil the peasant," answered the rabbi in a gruff voice. Then he entered the house. "I have wood to sell, very cheap," he said.

"I am a poor widow. Where will I get the money?" the woman asked, her voice weak and bitter.

"I'll give it to you on credit," replied the rabbi.

"How will I pay you back?" she moaned.

"I will trust you," said the rabbi.

"And who will light the fire for me?"

"I'll light it for you."

And with that, he put some wood in the oven, kindled the fire, and whispering penitential prayers, he covered the oven and quietly slipped out the door.

The man who had followed the rabbi that day eventually settled down in the village, and now, every year, when the people report that their rabbi has made his annual trips to heaven on their behalf, the newcomer adds quietly, "Heaven? And maybe higher, too."

But even those of us who have not achieved the purity of heart of the rabbi of Nemirov can put our deeds to work as grist for the mill to improve our soul-traits. As Rabbi Perr explained it to me, if our motives are mixed or impure, or even false, just by trying to act in a good way we can come to a truer place. "A person can be in a situation where he fools himself into thinking he is saying or doing what he believes, but then will come a time when he will be tested on that, and through the test, he will indeed eventually be able to be what he espouses, so it doesn't remain only an external show."

What I draw from this is that Mussar isn't telling us to wait until we have become perfected inwardly before acting in the outer world. In fact, the tradition draws the opposite conclusion, and advises us that acting to uplift the world should be seen as a necessary step on the route to our own holy perfection. The Yiddish novelist Chaim Grade says it in a nutshell through words he puts into the mouth of one of his characters, a Mussar student who says: "Indeed, one can't reform the world if one isn't perfect. But one can't become perfect if one doesn't stand up for the wronged."

I can see how this works in the mundane events of my own life. One day, after Mussar had already worked its way well into my consciousness, I was working and didn't want to be disturbed. When the doorbell rang, I grudgingly got up to answer it, only to find on my doorstep a man with unfocused eyes, carrying a white cane. In his hand he held three scenic calendars, which he was selling not on behalf of any charitable organization but to supplement his own disability pension. I didn't need a calendar. I like to support responsible organizations. I don't like being solicited on my own doorstep. I had just gone shopping and had almost no cash. It wouldn't have been very hard for me to come up with any number of justifications for saying, "Not today," wishing him well, and heading back to work. Where I got stuck was on not wanting to be that way. Those just aren't the qualities I want to see in me or the world. When that became clear in my own mind, I knew I had to try to bring my actions into line with my ideals, and so I bought a calendar.

And so we are taught that our deeds have the remarkable power not just to help others, but also to make ourselves better. Improving ourselves like this makes the world a better place in two ways: we've still helped others *and* we've brought more virtue to life on earth by building up the divine qualities in our own soul.

Mussar appeared to me first as an entirely introspective discipline, and while that perception remains largely true, I've come to appreciate that it doesn't tell us that pursuing a spiritual life means we should turn away from our social responsibilities. Rabbi Salanter emphasized this neatly in a saying that is one of my favorites among the many he uttered: "Spiritual life is superior to physical life, but the physical life of another is an obligation of my spiritual life." The spiritual is unquestionably the priority, but stepping up to help others in their basic physical, human needs is an imperative for anyone who aspires to a spiritual life. It's not an option; it's an obligation.

At various times Rabbi Perr has been involved with social agencies and activities, and yet, in the Mussar way, his public actions can't be separated from his motives for self-improvement. I can recall more than one occasion when he discussed his frustrations with one public body or another, not in terms of its shortcomings but rather in regard to his own need to develop patience and restrain his tendency toward anger. When he told me the story I related above about Rabbi Salanter's efforts in the cholera epidemic, he ended it by saying, "Reb Yisroel talked about this event for the rest of his life. You know what he talked about? That he lost his temper once in those stressful days. He saw it as a test for himself too, to test his own character, and he saw that in one case he had failed the test, and he talked about that, so others could learn."

Rabbi Perr pointed me to one other source that had influenced his own approach to this question of the relationship between inner work and outer work. In his daily *shmoozes* in the yeshiva, he often teaches from the book written by his wife's great-grandfather, the Alter of Novarodock, who founded the Mussar lineage he has inherited. In the last section of that book, the Alter states that engagement in community service is a prime way to lift the qualities of our interior life toward perfection. Then he goes even farther. "The only true index to the proper functioning of character," he says, "is community service; for in that [activity] the situation itself calls for the implementation of certain traits, or their contraries . . . If one wholeheartedly dedicates himself to community service, the community effectuates the fulfillment of his character potential, in due proportion, great or small . . ."

I've seen in my own life how engagement with social concerns provides me with not only a mirror that casts back a very accurate reflection of my own soul-traits, but also with an opportunity to work on those traits whenever challenges present themselves. In fact, I've come to see that anybody who wants to help the world has a virtual obligation to work on his or her own inner qualities, because any unconscious biases or untempered emotions that skulk in our dark inner reaches will inevitably hitch a ride out into the world on the backs of our well-intended deeds, there perhaps to work subversion, even against our own very best efforts.

Since my involvement with Mussar studies and practice, I have become more motivated to try to heal some aspects of the world around me. I have no illusions that I am going to be able to save the world, but it does seem to me that there are things I can do to affect the outcome of issues that are important to me. As I set about these activities, I keep a firm eye on the soul-traits I am putting into my actions, and on what I can learn from the way the world responds to me. Some examples might help clarify how this works.

I live in a part of the world that is rich in forests and ocean life. But big business is devastating the ancient rainforests, and the oceans are being overfished to depletion. I want to do something about this, but with Mussar now implanted deeply as a way of seeing myself and how I am in the world, I can't simply go out swinging in righteous indignation. I have to look within myself to see how I can be engaged with this pressing issue in a way that will bring more light to myself and to the world.

This introspection has led me to identify a number of soul-traits that might come into play in this sort of social action. Anger at those who are draining our world and the world of our grandchildren for their own financial benefit is certainly one of them. And when I probe this feeling, I can tell that if it were allowed to grow unchecked within me, anger would have the potential to blow up into violence, fanaticism, and destruction, as it so commonly does.

When I identify anger as the root of my motivation to bring good into the world, I see the contradiction. And I see a potentially incendiary outcome. Whether that means I burn myself up or I set fire to something or somebody else, the world just isn't going to be better for that action.

The alternative that I see is for me to home in on the soul-trait of compassion. Passing directly from anger to compassion for people whom I see as ignorant and selfish is realistically too hard a route for me to travel, so I focus instead on arousing compassion for the creatures that are the true victims of these human predators. When I think of sea lions shot for venturing too close to a salmon farm, or forest creatures losing their homes to loggers, my heart easily fills with compassion. Then, using that compassion as the starting point, I turn my mind and heart toward the humans who have done this. Suddenly, because the motivating quality is so different, I can feel that any practical action I now take will be founded on an inner quality that inspires hope—hope for me, for the task I have taken on, and for the outcome.

This Mussar-inspired approach works on a much more practical and personal level as well. I help to guide a small environmental group, one of whose members suddenly announced that she wasn't going to be able to carry through on her commitment to coordinate an event. My initial reaction was one of pure anger, and I immediately felt compelled to let everyone know how undependable this person had proved herself to be. But because my Mussar learning and practice have incrementally cranked open a space between emotional triggers and reflex reactions, I was able to retain enough awareness to see that responding in that angry way just wasn't what I really wanted. I didn't want to lay my anger on her, I didn't want to see that quality in me, and I certainly wouldn't choose to be visited by the bitter regret that always descends on me sometime after my anger is spent. And as those thoughts pushed the balance from rage to reason, I felt a little satisfaction creeping in, and I watched the *yetzer ha-ra* retreating back around the corner.

You know, I then thought, it's really unusual for someone to drop the ball like that for no good reason. Maybe there's some explanation for what happened. And so, with curiosity and concern but no longer any anger, I asked her about what was going on in her life, and then it all tumbled out—the broken relationship, the abuse, other problems, all adding up to a crisis. She was falling apart.

Without Mussar training and the perspectives it brings, in all likelihood I would have been just one more person dumping fuel on an already raging fire. Instead, I can say to myself that in this situation at least I did no harm, and maybe even made a little contribution toward her healing. And instead of indulging in one of those emotionally charged battles that so typically afflict any group, we quickly set about solving our problem and making sure the event went off as planned.

I can think of many other times someone's pushed my emotional buttons, whether it's my wife, my children, or just a crazy, aggressive driver I've met out on the road. I can't claim to have a perfect record in always rising up to the ideal response, but I have seen enough impact from my Mussar training to convince me that the practice effectively reduces enslavement to habit-bound reactivity, and at the same time increases our freedom to choose a course of action. And so now, whenever I rub up against other people, as inevitably happens, I recognize that every interaction presents me with another opportunity to learn about my soul-traits and to do some of the practice that may inch them one more notch toward where I'd like them to be. In my life, I haven't come across a more effective way to make a true difference—in the world within as well as the world without.

OPENING THE GATE

PRACTICING RIGHT SPEECH

Although our focus in this chapter has been primarily upon our actions in the world, what we say can often have as profound an effect on others—as well as on ourselves—as what we do. Had I acted on the anger I felt toward the woman who let down our group, for example, it's almost certain my reaction would have taken the form of harsh and biting words. Speech stands right at the threshold between thought and action, and so it partakes of both. With this understanding, Mussar makes "purity of tongue"—or "right speech," as it's called in Buddhism—an important focus of the work we do to elevate and balance our soul-traits.

Luzzatto writes that "our sages screeched like cranes about the promiscuous use of lips and ears," because damaging speech is equivalent to killing three people: it destroys the reputation of the victim, damages the perceptions of the listener, and diminishes the standing of the speaker. The impact is felt at the level of soul.

Wrong speech, *lashon ha-ra* in Hebrew, or literally "the evil tongue," can be any form of damaging or derogatory communication. It's wrong if it causes harm, or even stress, whether physical, financial, social, or psychological. It doesn't matter whether the statement is actually true or not, negative or not, secret or not. It doesn't matter if the person himself would say the same thing, were he asked. It's worse if the information also contains falsehoods, but that's not the most important point. Rather, we are being warned not to say anything with the intention—conscious or not—of damaging or belittling someone else and then taking pleasure in his disgrace.

Disparaging speech can be very tempting. Not only does it give us a sense of power because we demonstrate control of information and stand in judgment of others, it also can keep us from examining our own shortcomings. Condemning someone else as a tightwad or a drunk, or whatever, distracts us from spending that time and energy working on ourselves. But perhaps the most dangerous aspect of wrong speech is that it creates divisiveness among people—psychologically, emotionally, and socially.

Mussar gives us two ways to deal with wrong speech. The first is to abstain from it in the first place, but if we should slip, it shows us what we need to do to make amends.

Mussar construes abstinence in general to be an important form of practice. Holding ourselves back is seen as an effective way to prevent taking to excess our God-given healthy needs to eat, drink, speak, procreate, and so on. As is typical of Mussar, the directive is toward moderation. We are advised to participate in these sorts of activities only to the level that is necessary for good health and well-being, and to reject the temptation to take them any further.

In regard to speech, I think it was Sam Levinson who said, "It's not so hard to be wise. Just think of something stupid to say and then don't say it." The more formal guideline comes from Ecclesiastes: "There is a time to be silent and a time to speak." Curbing our speech may be difficult, but it is certainly less difficult than indulging "the evil tongue" and then having to clean up the mess we have created.

A story to illustrate this point is told about a man who said some terrible things about someone else. When he realized what he had done, he went to his rabbi for guidance. The rabbi thought a bit and then told the man to fetch a feather pillow. When he returned, the rabbi told him to go outside, rip open the pillow, and shake out the feathers. The man did as he was told. The wind caught the feathers and sent them flying. The man came back to the rabbi and said, "I did what you asked. Now what?" "Now go back outside and collect all the feathers," the rabbi replied. The man looked at him, dumbfounded. "How can I do that?" he asked. "The wind has taken them and who knows where they've gone." "Exactly," the rabbi said. "Just like your words. Once they're out, it's impossible to get them back."

In the Mussar tradition, the authority on this subject is Rabbi Israel Meir Kagan, better known as the Chafetz Chaim, who wrote several books on the rules of speech. His basic guidelines were:

1. Don't say derogatory things about anyone, whether they are true or not.
2. Don't imply derogatory things about anyone.
3. Don't listen to derogatory things about anyone, and if you do, don't believe them.

But because Mussar recognizes that most of us are not yet perfect, it also provides a mechanism for repairing the wrongs we will inevitably cause through speech. The actions that are recommended to rectify wrong speech are the same as those for all missteps between man and God:

1. Feel regret for the improper action.
2. Confess privately before God.
3. Commit yourself not to repeat the act.

If, however, the speaker's words have caused their subject some real physical, emotional, or financial damage, he must first ask forgiveness from the one he has offended. Once such forgiveness is obtained, what remains is the spiritual aspect of the offense that exists between man and God, which the speaker can address by following the steps outlined above.

There is an obvious tendency to couch guidelines for right speech in the negative: *Don't! Don't! Don't!* But another way to look at this issue is through the positive role that silence can play in our lives. Sitting in on Jewish ritual will immediately make it plain that silence is a scarce commodity in the Jewish world. There is only a brief part of the prayer service that is meant to take place in silence, and it too is filled in with prescribed words, even if these are said individually and quietly. But the practice of observing periods of simple silence appeals to me. I know how altogether differently I feel after a ten-day silent meditation retreat, when the break from the relentless and petty inner chatter clears the way for thought and perception to operate with uncommonly pristine clarity. I was overjoyed, then, to discover that Mussar acknowledges silence as a bona-fide spiritual practice. The classic book *Orchos Tzadikkim* devotes an entire gate to silence, and in it the anonymous author offers this advice: "Just as when one makes a door for his house, he has a time to open it and a time to keep it closed, so should one keep closed the doors of his mouth. Just as you would guard silver, gold, and pearls in your room, within a case, making one enclosure around another, do the same with your mouth."

Take a walk in silence, maybe with a friend. Spend even an hour at home committed to not speaking, just letting the telephone calls go to the voicemail. It may feel very odd at first if you are not used to it, because for most of us, running on at the mouth is a comfortable habit. Practicing silence takes courage, because we can't be sure what will bubble up into the space we open when the chatter stops, but see if after even a brief period of silence you don't feel more concentrated and self-contained, and in touch with deeper inner truths. Sometimes we chatter on just to avoid uncomfortable realities that lurk just under the threshold of consciousness, but that only holds them at bay, it doesn't deal with them. Whatever may come into the silence, we can be sure that it lives in us and we would do well to deal with it.

In fact, silence can open the door to great insights. The author of *Orchos Tzadikkim* tells us that, next to the lessons of a master, silence is the best teacher we can find. "If you cannot find someone to teach you Mussar," he writes, "cleave to silence."

CHAPTER NINE

THE GATE OF
THE DUTIES OF
THE HEART

"If one does acts of loving-kindness to a friend, it is accounted to him as if he built the world."

—YEHIEL BEN YEKUTIEL,

SEFER MA'ALOT HA-MIDDOT

Contributing to our community in ways that assist our own soul on its journey of ascent is surely one of the most important ways Mussar offers to teach us how to elevate our spirituality without removing ourselves from the here and now. But for me, the ultimate test of any spiritual practice has always been, and still remains, whether it gives rise to more caring and deeper love in our personal relationships.

The Mussar teachers have always emphasized the importance of bringing their own practice to their most intimate relationships. Observing how we act toward a spouse, a partner, children, parents, and good friends can give us an accurate reflection of the state of our soul-traits, and the chances are good that if one of these traits is in need of attention, it will make itself known in the mirror of our closest relationships. But, thankfully, the opposite is also true. How far we have come on Mussar's path of transformation can also be measured in how much more kindly and caring we are toward those whom we love.

There is a story told about a Mussar rabbi that clearly illustrates this point. The rabbi's talk was running late one Friday afternoon, and his wife opened the door to the study hall just a crack and whispered, "They have wives."

At that the rabbi started to cut short his talk, but one of the students protested. "Our wives don't mind," he said.

"First of all," the rabbi replied, "I don't believe you, and you cannot speak for them. Second, your wives are hungry and it is not correct to delay their meal." He then led the group in a rapid final prayer, wished them each "Good Shabbos," and sent them home.

Many stories like this one have come down to us, because Mussar is nothing if not a practical discipline based on watching our steps in the everyday world. This point was made real to me in a very personal way during one of my later visits with Rabbi Perr.

He had long ago cautioned me not to allow my seeking to draw me away from my wife and family. I knew what he meant. By that time, Bev and I had been married twenty-seven years. We'd lived in England and India, and we'd raised two daughters. Over the course of those many years, our ideas about life and living had evolved jointly, but now I was not only away in New York a lot of the time, I was also learning and growing in ways that did not include her.

Because we'd always shared so much of our lives and

thoughts, and because I didn't want this new path I was exploring to put a wedge between us, I became anxious to create an opportunity for Bev to meet Rabbi and Mrs. Perr in their world in Far Rockaway. And, having heard so much about them, Bev looked forward to meeting them, too. So when Mrs. Perr suggested that she come join us for a weekend, I quickly made the arrangements. Bev's fiftieth birthday was coming up and a weekend in New York—half in Far Rockaway, half in Manhattan—sounded like an ideal way to celebrate.

On the appointed weekend, I was already in Far Rockaway and Bev was scheduled to leave home on Friday morning and reach New York at about 6:30 P.M. that same day, well ahead of sunset and the start of the Sabbath, which was due to arrive at about 8:00 P.M.

In all Orthodox communities, the Sabbath is a day of total disengagement from ordinary activities. The injunction that governs the day is to rest, and as a result, the list of prohibited activities—working, cooking, shopping, driving, laundering, writing, gardening, and so on—is very long. Looking in from the outside, the thought of so many restrictions might make observing the Sabbath seem a terribly inconvenient burden, but the reality is sweetly the opposite. As the hours of Friday tick by, a palpable ripple of anticipation passes through the community. People meeting on the street invariably wish one another "Good Shabbos." Students are dismissed from the yeshiva at noon, and everyone rushes about doing their final shopping and food preparation. Timers (like the one whose buzzer Rabbi Perr had lamented to me) are set to operate lights and appliances.

And then, as the day's light fades from the sky, the week's cares and worries wane with it, and an unburdened, luminous spirit begins to stir. All preparations have been made, nothing more can be done, and the soul is invited to disengage from its worldly bindings and rise up within us. In the evening ritual that ushers in the Sabbath, the day is likened to a bride, who is welcomed by her loyal and loving family.

When I arrived at the Perrs' home on the Friday of my wife's visit, it was six o'clock, and since I hadn't heard from her, I knew it was safe to assume she'd left Vancouver on time. But at six-thirty the phone rang. Bev had had to change planes in Toronto, and that's where she still was, sitting locked on the plane, waiting on the ground for clearance. Apparently, thunderstorms en route to New York were the cause of the problem. She had no idea when they would take off, and there was nothing she could do but sit tight and wait.

That was okay, I told her. So long as they took off within the next half hour, she'd still make it just under the wire for the Sabbath. Everything was ready for her visit, and I was happily anticipating seeing her so soon, and having her meet the Perrs. But at seven o'clock the phone rang again. Still on the ground, and still no sign of movement.

At that point Rabbi Perr suggested that if she didn't want to breach the Sabbath by traveling, she could get off the plane and spend the day in Toronto, and then come to New York after that. But, as she'd already told me, the doors were locked. So she was coming, no matter what, and clearly there was no way she'd reach Far Rockaway before sundown. Suddenly this visit, which had been intended to bring together the two most important parts of my life, was beginning to get tricky.

Then Rabbi Perr had a brainstorm. Bev would be landing at LaGuardia Airport, and his daughter lived very close by. It was still possible that Bev could get to her home before the Sabbath, and if I left now, I could meet her there. Then we could all re-unite on Saturday evening and have all day Sunday together. It wasn't perfect by any stretch of the imagination, but if the Sabbath was to be preserved, at least it was a plan.

But just then Bev called again, and when I explained that new proposal, she started to cry. This wasn't at all what we'd planned, and she hadn't spent so many hours traveling and worrying just to celebrate her birthday weekend with strangers on the other side of the continent. Two things were now abundantly clear: Bev wouldn't arrive before sundown, and she wasn't going to the rabbi's daughter's house.

At that point I came up with yet another option, which was that I could meet Bev at the airport, and spend Saturday with her in New York City, but that wasn't on Rabbi Perr's agenda either. "When she comes," he now instructed me to tell her over the phone, "she should find a non-Jewish taxi driver. That shouldn't be too difficult. Tell her to pay him in advance, and to put all her things into her suitcase. Ask her to arrange for the driver to carry her bags to the car and from the car into the house." I relayed all this to Bev, who agreed, and then I reminded her that after sun-down, no one in the Perrs' house would answer the phone. She'd be on her own until she arrived.

At that, Rabbi Perr and I, along with his youngest son, Mordechai, who was visiting from Israel, walked back to the yeshiva for evening prayers. As we walked along, Rabbi Perr ex-plained to me various rabbinical dictums on calculating the ex-act time to mark the beginning of the Sabbath. "Some opinions are more lenient than others," he said. When we returned home, it was nine o'clock and there was still no sign of Bev.

"I've lit candles for Beverly, too," Mrs. Perr informed me as we all retired to the living room to wait. Mrs. Perr's mother, who had been helped downstairs from her second-floor bedroom, sat at the dining table in the next room.

"We should eat," I suggested, "since there's no way of knowing when Bev will get here."

"Are you hungry?" Mrs. Perr asked.

"It's not that. It's just that I feel bad making everyone wait."

"So we'll set a time," Mrs. Perr replied. "If she's not here by then, we'll go ahead without her. How about ten o'clock?" she asked, directing her question to her husband. He nodded. Fine. I noticed how august he looked in the long, midnight-blue satin coat he wore only on the Sabbath.

We chatted, but I was feeling so awkward and uncomfortable at this point that it was hard for me to concentrate. Poor Bev was stranded out there somewhere. And when I thought about the entrance she would hopefully soon make, I kept envisioning that taxi driving up the silent street and stopping in front of the rabbi's house. I could see curtains surreptitiously being peeled back, and the reflection of the street lights in the neighbors' eyes as they peered out their windows.

"Mommy," Mordechai suddenly asked, "shall I sing to Bubby?" This handsome and strapping young man in his early twenties was asking if he should sing to his grandmother.

"Sure," his mother answered, "why not?"

Mordechai moved over to sit close to his grandmother, and with only the accompaniment of his hands tapping on the table, he began to sing in Yiddish. I could pick out bits and pieces of the song, especially the chorus, which repeated the words *"Shabbos koidesh"*—holy Sabbath. It told of all the activities going on in all the houses all over the world to prepare for the day of rest. The dough was being kneaded and the house cleaned, the food was being prepared and the wicks on the lamps trimmed. As he sang, his Bubby rocked her head from side to side, and occasionally mouthed some of the words.

When Mordechai's song ended, we all savored a few moments of silence. An uncommon gentleness soothed the air. Then I looked at my watch. It was ten o'clock and still no Bev.

Mrs. Perr invited us all to come to the table. Rabbi Perr made the blessing over the wine, and, after we had washed our hands, he blessed the bread, and then the first course was served. We found things to talk about, but the unmentioned focus of everyone in the room was clearly the absent Bev.

"Will she be able to find the place?" Mrs. Perr finally asked. I assured her that Bev was an experienced traveler, and that wouldn't be a problem, but even I felt only partially reassured.

Then Rabbi Perr asked, "How will she feel when she gets here?"

I expect she'll feel terrible, I told him. She'll feel bad about disrupting the Sabbath, and awkward and embarrassed at how she had started off this first meeting with people who were so important in my life. And, because she was unfamiliar with the ways of Orthodoxy, she'd have no idea what kind of reception to expect. I was sure she'd be pretty miserable about now, if she was feeling anything at all like I was.

"So, it's our job to cheer her up," Rabbi Perr stated with conviction. His face creased into one of his sparkling but poignant smiles, and his eyes seemed to be telling me that life is full of sorrows but it's still a wonderful gift. I felt my spirit lift for the first time that evening.

About ten minutes later there was a knock at the door. Mrs. Perr flew up, and by the time I reached the front hall, she had her arms around Bev. Everyone crowded around, making sure she was okay. Then she was ushered to the table like the Sabbath Bride who'd been only a little delayed. No one mentioned the time.

The things that had happened that evening certainly weren't easy for Bev or me, and they weren't easy for the Perrs either. At one point, Rabbi Perr had called the whole situation "a nightmare." People who follow Orthodoxy consider observing God's commandments to be their primary responsibility in life, and honoring the Sabbath is one of the very highest priorities. But, forced into a situation where there were no good choices, and circumstances were beyond their control, the Perrs didn't get so overwrought that they allowed themselves to forget to be loving and kind. Those who practice Mussar are not only enjoined to be kind, they are taught to cultivate the love of kindness. That, too, is one of the divine commandments.

Ibn Pakuda titled his book *The Duties of the Heart,* and uses that phrase to describe those rabbinical commandments that are to be performed where only the inner eye can see, such as trusting in God and being introspective. I take the liberty of giving the phrase a little broader meaning, to refer to those situations on the spiritual path where we are well-advised to lead with the heart and to see the importance of the hearts of others as we set about cultivating our own. I'm speaking, of course, of the personal relationships in our lives.

One of the great gifts Mussar has given us is its detailed descriptions of all the human virtues, those traits of the cultivated soul that reflect the Divine attributes. High up on every list of these virtues is love, and of the many possible kinds of love, the highest, of course, is love of God. But that can be an abstract and remote ideal, and Mussar, in its practical realism, shows us how to work with our own experience in order to model and develop this virtue.

We are told to love people not for our own gratification nor for theirs, but because people are cast in the image of the Divine, so that when we love another person, we are also practicing for the ultimate act of love. When we love our dear ones, we honor them and the One in whose image they are made, and that helps to foster love for the One.

But how we manifest that love matters as well. What we hold in our hearts is important, but the only test that can assure us we are not fantasizing or deluding ourselves is to put our convictions into action. It may be easy enough to think silently, "I love you"; a bit harder to speak the words aloud. But it is most challenging, and ultimately of greatest benefit to the development of our soul-traits, to practice love in deeds, especially if we see before us pain and need, in whatever form.

This kind of love is called in Hebrew *chesed*, which translates as "loving-kindness." Sometimes this virtue is interpreted simply as a matter of fulfilling social obligations, such as giving charity, visiting the sick, helping the homeless. But it is possible to do these sorts of good deeds, and in fact be very helpful, while still missing entirely the spiritual basis for such acts. When we help others, we have the opportunity not just to improve their well-being but also to pay attention to the impact our acts have on our own soul. If our response comes out of a closed heart, we are left with a closed heart; if we struggle to reach for a higher truth, we are gifted with the imprint of that higher quality on our soul. And it is our closest relationships that offer us the most accessible—and maybe the hottest—flame with which to temper our inner nature.

Rabbi Perr, like all Mussarists, places tremendous emphasis on the tests that we can seek out in life, or that life throws our way. The exercises we are guided to practice in isolation are like laboratory tests, undertaken only as preparation for those we'll encounter outside the lab. As Moishe Broide said to me that night at dinner, "Studying Mussar is nothing. You must *do* Mussar." Or, in the words of Rabbi Perr, we must at some point graduate from theory to practice.

Rabbi Perr told me a story one day that left even him shaking his head in astonishment at the capacity of the human heart to love and serve.

"When I was teaching at my father-in-law's yeshiva," he said, "a man showed up one day unexpectedly. His wife had snapped, unfortunately. She was having a psychotic episode, and she was screaming like a banshee. With tremendous energies! Madperson energies! She was screaming without stop, without eating, without resting, without sleeping, around the clock. And she had to be restrained from jumping out the window, from attacking people. Can you imagine?

"Now, this man didn't want to hospitalize her because he was afraid of the stigma. And he knew there was a doctor in Flatbush who gave shock treatments in his office. He had arranged to see this doctor, but he had to wait to take her there. There would be a series of treatments, and she would have to be kept not too far from Flatbush until the treatments took effect. So they wound up in my father-in-law's apartment.

"Three or four of my students, who were in their twenties, and me too, we took turns guarding her so she wouldn't harm herself or jump out the window. And the whole time she was spewing obscenities.

"This fellow had been taking the whole load on himself. He'd been up with her around the clock for about a week. He hadn't changed his clothes, he hadn't eaten, he couldn't leave her alone. He was perspiring through his clothing, which was stained and filthy. He was a clean-shaven person and he hadn't shaved for a week. He was just a wreck.

"I said to him, 'How long has this been going on?' 'About a week now,' he answered. 'But how could you take it?' I asked. And you know what he answered me? He said, 'What do you think marriage is? Just for the good times?' Then after a moment he added, 'And how does God "take" *us*? That is also a marriage.' "

When he finished, Rabbi Perr sat and shook his head, but stories like this one abound in the lore of Mussar. They tell us that the soul in need right in front of us is a precious and vulnerable presence, and that meeting such a one can offer us a matchless opportunity to do the work we need to do on our own soul. Just as we are sustained, principally by powers beyond our control, so can we cultivate the practice of passing on that gift of sustenance. One of my favorite stories on this subject is told about Rabbi Israel Salanter.

Once, so it goes, when the Jews of Salant were gathered in the synagogue to begin the prayers for Yom Kippur, the most sacred day of the Jewish calendar, the rabbi was nowhere to be found.

Someone was sent to knock at his door, but there was only silence. Finally, as the sun was setting, the congregation could wait no longer to begin their prayers.

Just as the last few people were ending their devotions, Rabbi Salanter appeared, took his usual place, and began his prayers. Even though the others finished well ahead of him, he prayed through to the end. When he finished, he offered an explanation for why he had been so delayed.

He had been on his way to synagogue when he heard a baby crying. He had followed the cries to a house, and knocked on the door. There was no answer, so he tried the door, found it unlocked, and entered to discover a six-year-old girl asleep on the floor next to her wailing baby brother. Rabbi Salanter guessed that the children's parents had gone off to synagogue, leaving the older child with responsibilities beyond her years. He reported that he had fed the baby, organized his blankets, and put him back to sleep. Then he had awakened the little girl and told her to watch her brother. When she said that she was afraid to be left alone, he had stayed with the children until their parents returned.

Stories like this one tell us that taking care of the heart of another person is, in and of itself, an important and elevating spiritual act. We are directed to see the needs of others as opportunities for us to turn our spiritual commitments into deeds. That attitude will keep us focused on this reality, and will make us sharply aware of the choices we can make about how we conduct ourselves, which is the central impulse of the Mussar path.

And yet, we must be careful not to take away from these stories the idea that we get to perform these duties of the heart only in such dramatic circumstances. On the contrary, when we have internalized the attitude that will have us acting on these duties, we will find that it permeates all our personal relationships, from the most intense to the most incidental.

For example, it is the custom at the end of Friday evening services for all the men to line up and pass by Rabbi Perr to offer their Sabbath greeting. On one occasion, a young man stood in the line shepherding before him a boy of about four. When they reached the place where Rabbi Perr stood, the boy looked up at the tall rabbi and, with a distinct note of challenge in his voice, asked, "Who are you?" Without missing a beat, Rabbi Perr looked down at him and replied, "I'm Yechiel," giving the boy his first name, and then he asked back, "And who are you?" He didn't chastise the boy for what could, after all, be considered disrespect, and he didn't embarrass the man who was with him. By his matter-of-fact response, he was performing a simple kindness.

I should add here that I didn't actually witness this interchange. I was told about it by one of the older men at the yeshiva, who obviously considered it an incident worth repeating.

It's unlikely that Rabbi Perr would have told me this story himself, and not just because he wouldn't have considered it in any way extraordinary. He very seldom used stories from his own life to illustrate the path to a virtuous life. He would relate occasional amusing personal stories, certainly, and he never hesitated to discuss his weaknesses and challenges. But he held to the *middah* of modesty, and was genuine in not presenting himself as a model to be emulated.

So it was surprising to me, when we were discussing the importance of cultivating loving-kindness, that he told me about how he had used himself as an example in a conversation he'd recently had.

"I try not to speak about myself," he began, "but, much to my own surprise, I found myself speaking about myself to my son-in-law. I wanted to teach him an important thing, that when there is one family member who is acting as caregiver to an older person, it is awful when other people in the family participate only by coming to visit and getting brownie points for that, instead of helping.

"I told him that my own brother had taken care of my elderly mother. When I visited her, I never criticized my brother. I never said, 'Why don't you do it this way? Why don't you do it that way? Did you call the doctor for this?' And not, mind you, because I didn't have any criticisms. Then, when my brother arranged the funeral, I didn't like the way he was doing it, but I said to him, 'I'll go along with you because you took care of her when she was alive, so you are entitled to take care of her when she is dead.'

"Then he asked me if I would draw up a text for her tombstone, and I did. I worked hard at it, and I thought it was very good. He also drew up his own text, which I thought was inferior to mine, but again I said to him, 'Eliezer, you took care of her in her last years; you took care of the funeral; we'll put your text on the tombstone.

"I told my son-in-law that was the way to take care of a sibling who was taking care of a person, not coming along and telling him you had a better way to do it. Not questioning him. Not giving all kinds of advice. Go and pitch in and help the person; don't just sit down and take brownie points. I very rarely use myself as an example, but this time I felt I had to say, 'I do this myself,' and it is permitted to speak of yourself for this purpose. Not that I'm a greater person, or smarter, or more clever, but just to say, 'I do this myself.' "

Quietly he added, "Taking care of the caregiver is more important than taking care of the person."

I've learned a lot about the importance of caring, both from Mussar and directly from Rabbi Perr. That same evening, when Bev had finally arrived in Far Rockaway after her nerve-wracking trip, and after we had eaten and were at last enjoying each other's company just as I had dreamed we would, Rabbi Perr told us a story that demonstrated on more than one level the high priority he placed upon this beautiful quality of the human heart.

It involved a teacher he'd had as a teenager who was very strict about not allowing students who arrived late to enter the classroom. "If you were brave, you could knock; he might answer, or he might not. If he did, he might let you in, or he might not. He might just close the door right in your face. He was a wonderful teacher; he just didn't tolerate teenage sloppiness.

"So, one Friday, a boy named Pinchas knocked on the door. It was nine thirty-one. The teacher opened the door, looked out, then closed the door and returned to his class.

"When the class met again the following Monday, the teacher came in as usual, but before he began the lesson, he spoke to the boys. 'I didn't know that Pinchas is the son of a baker,' he said, 'and that he stays up all night on Thursdays helping his father bake for Shabbos. And, after working the whole night, he goes home, takes a shower, changes his clothes, and then rushes here to class.

" 'Pinchas,' he said, turning to address the boy, now with tears beginning to stream down his face, 'can you forgive me for not letting you into the class on Friday? Can you ever forgive me? I was so wrong.' "

By the time he finished the story, Rabbi Perr's eyes, too, were streaming with tears. And his voice caught as he said, "Can you imagine? The man cared that much!"

And while he told this story to illuminate the quality of loving-kindness, it was clear to me that he also wanted to relieve any feelings Bev might still be carrying about her unavoidable lateness, and so telling that story was Rabbi Perr's own quiet act of loving-kindness.

The remainder of our time together proved to be an affirmation of that quality, particularly among the Perr family, but also in the community at large.

On Saturday morning we all attended prayers at the yeshiva, where, as is customary, men and women were seated in adjacent rooms, the opening between them separated by a sheet. From time to time I could see the sheet being drawn back a crack, and Mrs. Perr pointing out to Bev where I was sitting.

In the afternoon, there was a bar mitzvah luncheon at which the Perrs were honored guests and we, as their guests, were also made welcome. The strict separation of men and women was more relaxed during these festivities, but still, for the most part, men visited with men and women with women. I kept an eye on Bev as Mrs. Perr took her around, introducing her to the other women and making sure she was never neglected. I could detect that Bev was a bit tense, attentively alert, and generally watching her step in this alien world, though no more than I had done at the beginning.

As we made our way back to the house later that day, through streets deserted of traffic, where families in their Sabbath finery strolled and greeted one another, enjoying not only this day of rest but also the warmth of early spring, Bev and Mrs. Perr were walking arm in arm.

Afterward, Bev told me how much she had enjoyed her time with these people. She genuinely appreciated the warmth and openness with which they had welcomed her into their home. In the course of the weekend, she'd abandoned most of the stereotypes she'd brought with her, especially concerning Orthodox women and their lives. Although it is true that men and women are considerably more separated in Orthodox society than in the world at large, and that, particularly in and around the yeshiva, men hold a preferred place, the women whom she met were anything but docile or cowed by the roles they had been assigned. In fact, many of them, like Mrs. Perr, were bright, educated, inquisitive, strong, and even outspoken.

Bev was touched by her time in Far Rockaway, and because of what she saw and experienced there, she became curious to learn more about Mussar. And the more she has seen the incremental changes this discipline has brought into my life, and through me into our life together, the more she has been supportive of my efforts to learn and practice.

OPENING THE GATE

REMOVING OBSTACLES THAT OBSTRUCT
THE FLOW OF LOVE

Someone once asked how the great wise ones differ from the rest of us. Are their souls filled with unconditional love, while ours are not? The answer came back that unconditional love is fully present in all our souls. The difference is that, in our case, there are many other qualities present as well, some of which obstruct the flow of that love.

Mussar directs us to pay close attention to these obstructions, and one of the ways it gives us to improve our soul-traits is to concentrate our efforts not on the trait we want to improve but rather on the opposite or contrary trait. In that way, as Rabbi Shlomo Wolbe puts it, "Your bad character traits will be erased by your good traits."

So, for example, if you were dealing with a tendency to be short-tempered, you could work on developing a discipline of good deeds or kind thoughts that would build up a counterbalance to your tendency to excessive anger. But the same also works in reverse: if you felt that the quality of love was not strong in your heart, you might work on diminishing your anger, which is one of the traits that can stand in the way of love.

As Rabbi Perr puts it, it is futile to try to improve ourselves simply by saying, "Don't!" We can never overcome anger just by saying, "Don't be angry." In general, Mussar discourages us from dealing with any soul-trait by trying to block it up or wipe it out, because that will be about as useful as telling a depressed person to cheer up. We know that without deeper change having taken place, as soon as a difficult or stressful situation arises again, we'll most likely fall right back into the negative habit we're trying to kick.

And, in any case, a trait like anger is not, in and of itself, a reprehensible quality. It is appropriate to be angry in certain circumstances, and the focus of the practice is therefore not to try to remove anger from our soul by pulling it out by its roots, but rather to adjust the level of our anger and our ability to express it appropriately, and to address other soul-traits that might be fueling the anger we feel.

Rabbi Perr shared with me some of the Mussar practices that are intended to help us with our anger, a trait he says most people are interested in dealing with because "they really regret later on being angry, because in anger we do foolish things."

The first step is simply to acknowledge that anger is a problem. "You first have to be aware that you don't want it. It's harming your health and your relationship with the person you're angry at. And you're going to regret it. It destroys the love in a family. A family can't function when there is anger."

"Next, you have to learn to recognize the signs of anger in yourself. You have to feel the anger rising in your gut." This step involves raising your level of awareness, which can be accomplished in several ways. Meditation can help, as can the "accounting of the soul" practice described in Chapter Five.

"When you feel it rising," Rabbi Perr went on, "you activate practices you have prepared that work to insert a space, so that the fuse isn't instantly ignited." Remember, you aren't telling yourself that you're not allowed to get angry. Rather, you focus your work on introducing a space of time between the triggering incident and your response. Mussar provides the resources to help us do that.

You might, for example, establish a rule that says you must wait until the next morning before expressing your anger, or that you may act out your anger—but only when you are wearing a particular pair of shoes, or only after drinking a glass of water.

Let's say one of your children is dawdling and making you late. You feel yourself getting angry. So before you open your mouth to say something, you have to remember to look down to check if you're wearing your "angry" shoes. Or you go to the sink and pour yourself a glass of water. Either of these actions will have pried open a little space between your awareness of becoming angry and your acting upon it. By doing this, you prevent consciousness from being blotted out or overwhelmed by a cloud of emotion—"not all locked up; imprisoned," Rabbi Perr put it—and you restore to yourself a measure of choice. But this does require a high degree of awareness, which has to be cultivated through practice.

Another approach to dealing with anger might be to work on another soul-trait that would help diminish it. There are usually several factors giving rise to any particular behavior. A person who felt he was not loving enough might come to realize that the level of his anger was a hindrance, but, probing deeper, he might find that his anger was actually being fueled by too much impatience. In that case, focusing practice on relieving impatience would have the effect of decreasing the symptom—anger—thus making more space for love.

One of Rabbi Shlomo Wolbe's favorite teachings is directed to helping people overcome impatience. He suggests that we commit to being patient for only thirty minutes each day, and he tells us to choose the thirty minutes that are the greatest challenge. Let's say, for example, that you come home from work every day to find your children screaming and crying. Your spouse, who is exhausted from taking care of the family all day long, has long ago lost patience and is screaming right back at them. So what do you do? Too typically, you start screaming too, adding your own fuel to the fire.

Rabbi Wolbe suggests that once you realize this pattern, you charge yourself to observe patience for the first half hour after you walk in the door. When you come home the next evening, you must be committed to entering the scene calmly and quietly. (You might try wearing a rubber band on your hand to remind yourself to do this!) You will say a few kind words to your harried spouse, "then pick up the first child, hold him and hug him, sing to him a little, and carry him slowly to his bed. Put him into his bed, still singing gently to him. In five minutes he will already be dozing off.

"Then you take the next child, and so on, until with your patience you have turned that half hour that you used to get angry all the time into the half hour when the house returns to quietude. Over time you will see how much more you can accomplish with patience than with anger."

After working with that half hour for a month, you can move to another half hour at some other time of day. And so, over a year, you will have learned patience throughout the day.

"After a year," Rabbi Wolbe says, "you will be so used to being patient in every situation that you will realize internally how much better patience is than anger. With so much experience with patience . . . you will respond patiently to whatever happens to you."

CHAPTER TEN

THE GATE OF
DEEP WITHIN

"It is clear that a considerable number of the motions of the psyche are concealed in the hidden chambers of a man's heart every day, one within another, so that he no longer knows or recognizes them. But the more deeply they are hidden, the more strongly do they act within the psyche."

—RABBI MENAHEM MENDEL LEFFIN,

SEFER HESHBON HA-NEFESH

My first visit had lasted only a day, then I had come for a weekend, followed by a few more visits of about a week, until I finally reorganized my life to spend a full month with Rabbi Perr in Far Rockaway. In that longer stretch of time my learning and my inspiration grew much deeper, and I felt sadness when the month drew to its close.

On my very last day, I was standing with some of the men at the yeshiva when someone, whom they all knew well, came up to the group and announced, "I have a question of *halacha*"— ritual law. With that, he immediately grabbed everyone's attention, because every day they all find themselves considering how decisions they are about to make fit (or maybe don't fit) within the complex traditional guidelines they strive to follow. And so they all turned to him and waited expectantly. He looked from one to the other before confiding his problem. "Do you think Steely Dan is a good enough group to break Shabbos for? They're performing this Friday evening, and..." Everyone rolled their eyes and laughed.

It was just such flashes of humanity—and humor—that opened up the environment and so allowed me to feel more at ease in that strictly Orthodox community than I could ever have imagined. It also helped that the men went out of their way to make me feel welcome. One Sabbath early on, as I stood in the prayer hall, frankly less engaged in prayer than in worrying about how I, in my ritual incompetence, might be about to trip up and embarrass myself publicly, the *gabbai* approached me. The *gabbai* is the man who stage-manages the ritual, making sure the right people are in the right place doing the right things at the right time. As he came toward me, I wondered what I could have done wrong. My heart pumped sludge.

"Can you dress the Torah?" he asked. That task involves no more skill than tying a strap around the scroll and sliding the cloth cover over the top. Yes, I could do that. And because being asked to do anything in relation to the Torah is an honor, I felt instantly touched and pleased that this congregation of men among whom I was an awkward stranger had acknowledged me in this way.

And so, in casual situations as well as in the formal circumstances of prayer and study, I found myself surrounded in Far Rockaway by people who lived with a vital connection to their ancient traditions, and yet who were, when all was said and done, still people, who saw in me too, when all was said and done, a person. And then I had the thought that this humanized environment might not exist in spite of, but rather as a result of, the religious discipline and teachings they had inherited, an inheritance that is the primary source of form and direction in their lives.

All of my experience in Far Rockaway had put into new perspective for me what it meant to be—and to live as—a Jew. Up to this point, most of my experiences of being Jewish had felt like trying to breathe at high altitude—in my usual, assimilated environment, it was a struggle just to get something good out of the thin air. Here, however, I felt I was breathing rich, pure oxygen. I had touched on something that was at once creakingly ancient—even older than history—and at the same time completely grounded in everyday life, and deeply real.

To live bound up with a functioning, sustaining human community has become a rare experience in our fragmented world, so it doesn't surprise me that, once I got over my initial discomfort, I found myself feeling gently held and firmly sustained by the fabric of life they had woven in that place. And yet, this same experience also offered me a challenge I couldn't ignore. These people were so deeply rooted and grounded in their particularity, so confident of where exactly they fit in, that I was forced to ask the same questions of myself. I had to consider, as I never had before, what it meant to me to be a Jew. What solid commitments was I prepared to make to my Jewishness—or to my life, for that matter? As was inevitable, I had even considered donning the fringes and giving myself over to the rhythms and rigors of the Orthodox life.

In the end, however, I had to acknowledge that the center of my life really lay elsewhere, and that it was time for me to leave. But I was also aware that, after so many significant experiences, certain aspects of my identity had effectively been uprooted, and as a result I could never go back to exactly the same life I had been living only months before. Undoubtedly there would be some tension ahead, but I felt prepared for that, and accepted it as the cost of change. And I reminded myself that, in any case, my central focus was still Mussar, and everything I had learned about Mussar told me that the real crucible in which to work the alchemy of elevation and transformation is the laboratory of everyday life. There was no one place on earth that would be better or worse for doing the inner work that lay ahead.

The power of that truth did not, however, manage to dilute the sadness I felt about leaving, though I consoled myself with the thought that, God willing, I would return to visit again in the future.

I had indicated to Rabbi Perr that I wanted to spend some time with him that last day, so I knew he'd be expecting me when I knocked on his office door and announced, "The *noodnick* is here," using the Yiddish term for "nuisance" that conveys a little kid's relentless nasal nagging, which distracts the entire world from its weighty concerns for the sake of a petty nothing.

He looked up, eyes smiling, and said dryly, "That doesn't identify you. Everyone around here is a *noodnick.*"

Glad to have it confirmed that I fit right in, I crossed to my chair and, aware of how little precious time remained to me that day, launched into the questions I had brought to discuss. What was uppermost in my heart and mind that day was to get a better understanding of how, according to Mussar teachings, we can use and deal with emotion in our spiritual lives.

"Reb Yisroel," Rabbi Perr began thoughtfully, referring to Rabbi Salanter, "and all the Mussar masters, used emotions as a way of reaching into people, to help motivate them. In Novarodock, a good Mussar *shmooze* always had to have either tears or laughter, and preferably both."

He paused for a moment, pulling on his beard, and then leaned forward, his elbows planted firmly on the papers on his desk. "Emotions can be a key to open up your inner world," he said, before embarking on a roundabout route to demonstrate his point. "You know," he continued, now leaning back once more, "lowbrows listen to CBS and they hear about the murders in Queens and Brooklyn. Highbrows listen to NPR and they hear about the murders in Kosovo and Rwanda. Why is that highbrow? Because it's farther away. Why is the person who is interested in the moons of Jupiter more of an intellectual than the person who is interested in which cat food his cat enjoys? It's big and it's far and it's impressive, but the sages say there is no big news of the day. There is no world. The world is you. It's all *narishkeit* [foolishness]. What's the difference whether it's in Rwanda or in Brooklyn? What's the difference? The whole world is filled with nonsense. Mist. Fog. There is no other world besides yourself."

While he retreated into his own thoughts for a moment, I reflected on how profound was that view of the interior and outer worlds. The connection to our topic seemed to be that if the only world I can know is what I myself experience, then all my inner states, including emotion, grow in significance, while the things of the outer world start to look like distractions.

Rabbi Perr called me back to the moment by taking off on another tack, now retelling the story of a time when the young Rabbi Salanter had followed his teacher to see what the older man did on his regular excursions into the woods surrounding their village. What he discovered was the teacher upbraiding himself in the silence of the deserted forest, calling himself names. " 'You thief! You nothing! You dope!' I'm not sure what he was calling himself," Rabbi Perr shrugged.

He was describing the practice of self-criticism that became a standard discipline within the Mussar movement. The exercise involves picking through your thoughts and actions with a fine-tooth comb and then—literally, verbally, and loudly—calling yourself to account for whatever weakness or misguided thinking or behavior you discover. Self-rebuke or self-reproof, it is called.

For me, this was one of the more difficult aspects of Mussar to accept. What, I wondered, could be the spiritual value in a person's berating himself like that?

Rabbi Perr explained. "Why was he doing this? Because the teenager who looks in the magnifying mirror and sees a little pimple becomes hysterical and is focused only on the pimple. But the parent says, 'But, dear, you're so beautiful! Why are you looking only at the pimple? Who notices such a little thing?' "

All of a sudden, he pulled back his head, raised his voice to a falsetto, and became a teenage girl. " 'Oh, it's so ugly! That little pimple is so awful.' Sniffle, sniffle. 'My face is ruined.'

"Right?" He looked at me for confirmation. "Because she doesn't want to tolerate even that small pimple. And a wise one does not want to tolerate even a small pimple of fault. And when he calls himself 'a *ganif*' [thief], he doesn't mean a thief who robbed a bank. He feels he is a *ganif* because he wasn't careful with someone else's money, or somebody else's object that he put down in a place where it could be harmed, or he didn't return the change, or he perhaps took an extra bag from the supermarket, or whatever it was that bothers him. And he doesn't want it to happen again, because he feels bad about it.

"So he goes where nobody can hear him, and he yells at himself, 'You *ganif!*' And he can't stand being called a *ganif,* because he has tried very hard not to be a *ganif.* So he is in pain, and that's going to help him not do this the next time.

"You're a *ganif!*" Rabbi Perr exploded so loudly and unexpectedly that I jumped. He caught his breath and then went on.

"So, that's what the exercise is doing. The exercise is *using* the emotions."

He removed his glasses and looked me right in the eye. "I am shocked when I open up a box of strawberries and I see that somebody has opened it up before me and pilfered it. And I've gone shopping and seen that someone has opened up a jar that is vacuum-sealed and taken out pickles and put the jar back on the shelf. What's the matter with these people? Weren't they taught right from wrong?

"I'm not a *ganif,* so if I found myself with such a weakness, I'd have to yell at myself. You *ganif!*" he boomed out, entering into the heightened emotion that is integral to the exercise. "You *ganif!* You *ganif!* You *ganif!* You *roshah* [evil person]!" His voice grew louder, and at the same time the tone of reproach and regret grew too. "You *ganif!* You *ganif!*" His voice rose to a scream and his cheeks flushed red. "You *ganif!* You *ganif!*" Then he started to choke, which put an end to his demonstration. I

195

couldn't help wondering what people hearing this display through the closed office door might have imagined was going on between us.

He caught his breath. "So, that's why you yell at yourself."

A practice like this can be powerfully transformative. "Like a blow," Rabbi Perr said. And its very power is what makes it also dangerous. It has to be used by just the right person in just the right way, and it certainly calls for the guidance and supervision of an experienced teacher. That way, its power will be directed toward positive and desired outcomes, not the potential self-destruction that can come from such forceful self-reproach.

"However, there's a however," Rabbi Perr went on, now turning to an issue that would take us deeper into the subject. "The however is that Reb Yisroel noticed it is possible in Mussar, even with *hispa'alus* [emotional fervor], for a person to take a phrase, and for him to review it and to repeat it to himself over and over again, until the words are illuminated in front of his mind's eye like a neon sign. And yet it has no effect on him! Reb Yisroel says it will not have effect until he goes down to discover what his flaw is that is causing this behavior.

"So whether it is reproaching yourself with emotion, or chanting with emotion, this is a contradiction. He contradicts himself!"

What's the contradiction? That Rabbi Salanter taught, on the one hand, that our soul-traits are rooted in the unconscious, beyond the range of the conscious mind, so that only those practices with the power to reach down into the inner darkness—like ones that involve heightened emotional states—are likely to achieve the deep reconfiguration we seek. But on the other hand, Rabbi Perr had quoted him as saying that this method might not work if the conscious mind isn't brought to an understanding of the source of any problem we are trying to address.

"I would explain it this way," he went on. "If a person has a real serious, habitual, psychological problem, he is not going to be able to overcome it just by *hispa'alus*. If he is, say, a kleptomaniac, and he tries to overcome it by calling himself a *ganif*, he's only going to break himself. A thing that is stronger than you, so to speak, that controls you, you can't gain control over it just like that. Then there has to be a totally different approach, and that is by finding another way into the fortress. You can't take it head-on, because it's in control. You've got to find out *why* you're doing what it is you're doing."

Rabbi Perr was always careful to stress, as had the Mussar masters before him, that this discipline is not intended to treat deep and extreme psychopathology. For the rest of us, though, who may not be so disturbed but yet are still aware of improvements we want to bring to our inner life, "for these people, it is possible for Mussar to help."

The issue Rabbi Perr was working to explain goes right to the core of Mussar thinking. Remarkably, at least seventy years before Freud, Rabbi Salanter understood that there are forces of what he called the inner *dunkel*, or darkness, at the very root of our being. And it is these forces or unconscious motivations that give rise to the conscious thoughts that shape the actions we perform in the light of day. He also observed astutely that the intellect is an inadequate and limited tool for excavating in that blackness, which is why he so strongly advocated using practices that didn't rely on thought—such as emotional chanting and self-reproof—as the dynamic tools of transformation.

But he was realistic and perceptive enough not to assign to

197

any one of our faculties a task it was not suited to perform, and so he also recognized that the power of emotional and other nonrational practices was limited as well. He concluded that extreme mental states were too strong to be uprooted by chanting and other Mussar methods. In those difficult cases, he saw that the conscious mind did have an important role to play, because identifying and acknowledging the source of the problem could be a first and important step toward change.

What this shows is that, although he was firm in saying that conscious thought was a weak agent to bring about profound inner change, he never demeaned the intellect as a useful faculty in its own territory. Since the sort of emotional practices he advocated presupposed awareness of which soul-traits a person was targeting, the intellect had a helpful role to play even in setting up the nonrational Mussar exercises. But more generally, as I explained in the discussion of the *heshbon ha-nefesh* practice (in Chapter Five), Mussar tells us that one of the most important things we need to do is to find ways—like *heshbon ha-nefesh*—to bring the contents of the unconscious into our conscious awareness. When our Mussar practice brings stuff from the darkness into the light of mind, that in itself works change in us, because to the extent that we are able to do that, our lives are no longer being directed by hidden inner forces.

Rabbi Eliyahu Dessler helps us get right to the essence of this important understanding of the Mussar way when he concludes that "the heart is cleansed of bias" when the seeker "has worked on himself to such an extent that he has achieved purity of heart. Then, and only then, is his insight clear and his judgment reliable. This work is what we call 'the work of *mussar.*' "

Following the chain of his logic will make this whole subject clearer. Bias, Rabbi Dessler tells us, leads us away from truth. So when any one of our soul-traits inclines too far one way or another, we are predisposed to meet the world through the screen of that bias. This interferes with our perception of truth. The solution for those of us who are not so unbalanced as to require even stronger medicine is to cleanse the heart, and for that job the intellect is just not a very effective tool. The intellect has its role, to be sure, but to help us touch the deep places where it cannot penetrate, Mussar calls on those of our natural faculties that have the power to reach over and behind the conscious mind to probe and affect the unconscious. That's why Mussar elects methods like emotional recitation, self-rebuke, melody, meditation, contemplation, and imaginative imagery as its favored tools to do the work of deep transformation.

Rabbi Perr looked at me intently, asking with his eyes if he had given me a clear explanation—which he had, and dramatically too—or whether there was anything else I wanted to talk about before I left.

In fact, I'd been rehearsing for a long time what I would ask from Rabbi Perr at this last moment to help me prepare for my return home. "I do have one final question," I said. "When you've spent time with a person, you tend to get a read on them, you know what I mean?" He nodded, and I went on. "So the question I want to ask you is, what guidance would you give me based on how you read me? That would be the most helpful thing I could carry away, I think, something that isn't led in any direction by my own questioning."

He thought for a moment, then he said, "You know, that's probably the most difficult question you've ever asked me."

"I saved it for last." I smiled.

"But to answer you," he went on, "I really have to know what you're looking for in yourself. If you tell me what you're looking for, I might be able to give you a little idea, because you're not the first one who has come past me this way. So, do you have an idea, or is it amorphous?"

It wasn't amorphous, that I knew, but I just didn't want to say anything that might influence his answer one way or the other.

"Because you don't want to tilt the pinball machine?" he asked.

Right. "I'd really like to know what you'd say based just on what *you* see in me. You must have some intuitive feelings," I persisted.

A smile played on his lips as he said, "I do have a couple of things I would like to say to you." He stroked his beard. "First of all, I think you have to make yourself a space, a space that is sanctified, around you. A space in time. It's hard, but it will automatically expand, because the way I see you, you're a person who is always in growth, which is rare, especially at your age— our age. You are growing. You know how to take care of yourself. You're pretty self-contained. I think you might be able to live on a desert island."

"That's not necessarily a virtue," I responded, thinking of the times my wife had railed at me for being a typically emotionally inaccessible male.

"In this case it *will* be a virtue," he answered. "I think that, if you cherish your space, you may discover others who start to intrude on it in order to share it, but they will only do that if you cherish it very deeply. Who will they be? I don't know. We shall see. I don't think you should push it. But you should hold that space very strongly. And the curtain around the space should be very obvious. If you make yourself a space, I think others will join you in the space, because I think the space is awfully attractive."

Then he went on to make his guidance specific by suggesting that I start to observe more of a Sabbath. I liked that idea, and it seemed like a practical way to try out what he had suggested. But that concrete suggestion wasn't all of what I heard him saying to me. Yes, observe the Sabbath, but in the curtain of separation he was proposing, I perceived his encouragement to be as strong as I could be in resisting the alluring blandishments of a society that enthralls us with its culture of consumption and distracts us from spiritual pursuits, thereby leading us away from our own best interests.

Just then the school principal came to the door. It was nearly time for me to go, but I had one more thing to ask of the rabbi, and so I gave him a beseeching look, and he responded by asking his colleague to come back in a few minutes.

"I don't know if this is appropriate," I began, once Rabbi Perr had refocused on me, "and I don't know if you do this, but I'm going to ask it anyway. Will you give me your blessing?"

He thought for a moment before answering. "In our world," he said quietly, "we don't give blessings." I was instantly disappointed, but he went right on. "But I will tell you this. God will pursue you. And that is the greatest blessing. You will find Him in the most unexpected places. He'll be there showing you that He is there. You are going to see His success in your undertakings and in your spiritual quest. He will pursue you, because you have done the first thing that is necessary: you have just opened the door. He's not going to let you go easily. God does not allow you to do insane things once you say, 'I am here, and I know You are there.' You'll see His hand as time goes on." And then he added, "And stay in contact." He might have meant with God, but I knew from the way he looked at me that he was inviting me to stay in touch with him.

"Is that a blessing?" he then asked. His face was radiant, reflecting the glow of the words that had poured from him. And he answered himself, with a thump on the desk, "A major blessing!"

In the few hours that remained before I had to head for the airport, I decided to see if I could find some sort of gift that might convey to the Perrs even a small token of the thanks I felt I owed them for having so generously made space for me in their lives.

I had seen that Rabbi Perr kept all his notes in longhand, so I chose for him the predictable pen. For the family, I got a cake from the house of kosher delights known as Zomick's Bakery, and on the box I wrote something about hoping the sweetness of the cake would echo the feelings for them that I carried away in my heart.

Bearing these gifts, I stopped at the Perrs' home to say my last good-byes. Rabbi Perr seemed genuinely touched by the cake. "Look," he said to his wife, eyes dancing, face alight. "He's written something on the box. What does that make you think of?" When she seemed completely at a loss, he reminded her. "It's like that cake box I used to have that had written on it, 'Happy birthday to Yechiel, from Bob and Ray.' " He assured me that he really had owned such a box, although I could never get straight what circumstances might have brought together an Orthodox rabbi and a pair of classic radio comedians. The image boggled my mind.

And then it was time for me to go. Rabbi Perr took both my hands and looked deeply into my eyes with a love that reached back centuries. He brought his face close and kissed my cheek, his soft, warm hand cradling my neck. I didn't even try to choke back my tears. I knew then how deeply I had been touched. My life had begun anew, and I was so grateful.

Then I heard Mrs. Perr say, "Give him a good hug for me too, Yechiel." I wanted to throw the arms of my heart around both of them, but it was only him I was allowed to touch, so I made sure he could feel that I clasped him with enough love for two.

THE TRUTH OF
OUR STRUGGLE

*"The righteous have no peace, not in this world and
not in the world to come, as it is written, 'They
ascend from strength to strength.' "*

—PSALM 84; THE TALMUD

I t has been three years since I nervously climbed the steps to
the old building that then housed the Yeshiva of Far Rockaway. A new building, which was being banged and poured
into place during the time I was visiting with Rabbi Perr, has
since been completed. It has a large and modern study hall, class-
rooms, and offices, and I can only assume that this expansion and
modernization means I'm not the only one who has been drawn
to and touched by Rabbi Perr and his teaching.

As for me, I can happily report that I still live in the same
house, with the same wife and same children. I drive the same
old car and, mostly, I have the same friends. I sit and read and
write in the same study where my eyes were first opened to *The
Path of the Just* and *The Duties of the Heart.* Just reminding my-

self of those days brings back echoes of the raw pain that sent me off on this journey.

That's all a memory now. The dust has settled and time has done its magic, but more than anything, I can say that I have learned a new way of living, from the inside, that won't be very evident to anyone who looks at my house or my car or family.

It's funny to call it a "new" way of living, when you consider that the first Mussar book I read was written around 1050. Recently, as I was studying *The Palm Tree of Deborah,* a book first published in Venice in 1588, I found myself thinking, Oh, that's not so long ago. And, considering that human nature seems not to have changed in the slightest since we took up agriculture in the Euphrates Valley not many thousands of years ago, and that Mussar was initiated in the tenth century, it isn't.

Developing a personal bond to an ancient wisdom tradition—with which I've connected more deeply than I ever could with Hinduism or Buddhism—has been one of the biggest invisible changes I have made in my life. As a filmmaker I had come to see culture as anything that qualified for this year's award ceremonies, which meant it had been created within the previous twelve months, while everything else was history. Now I feel joined to a continuous stream of tradition reaching all the way back to the revelation at Mount Sinai, a transmission that was almost snuffed out for me in my parents' generation, but that I am now collecting and reassembling for myself, like an orphan putting together fragments of a treasured family photo. I'm still just a tiny scrap of color down at the bottom, but at least now I feel I am becoming part of a much bigger picture.

Plunking myself down, as I have done for periods of time, in the middle of an Orthodox community has given me a new appreciation for that particular version of the Jewish tradition, and has made me comfortable about finding ways to be more observant in my own life. Just as Rabbi Perr suggested, I've brought the Sabbath into my weekly schedule, and I've grown to love that time. Now, on a harried midweek day, as I race around doing the business of my life, if I see one of those bumper stickers that call out HANG IN, SHABBOS IS COMING, I nod and smile. A day of rest and disengagement is restorative of physical and psychic energy, but it is much more than that as well. By taking a calculated step back at a fixed time every week, I regularly open up space for gaining new perspectives on whatever happens to be going on in my life, which is something that wouldn't happen if I left myself constantly harnessed to and straining at my burdens. It's also a chance to taste at least a morsel of the holiness that Mussar tells us is our potential, and it's nothing less than a sacred mini-retreat where I take refuge every week.

Embracing the Sabbath means restrictions. I don't do any work, and I don't turn on my computer. I don't shop, no matter how hard my daughter begs. I avoid the phone. I have come to see and appreciate how taking on these voluntary restrictions gives me a frame within which to be thoughtful and creative in a way that absolute freedom and license just don't. Poets do something similar when they adopt the structure of the haiku or quatrain. Sure, they're rigid and restrictive, and free verse is so much more unbounded, but accepting a defined playing field has a way of freeing us up to concentrate on the inspiration and vitality that can flow as we struggle to express ourselves within the lines that have been drawn.

My family has joined me in making the Sabbath part of our

life, although at this point only to a degree. My younger daughter, Leora, at first had the hardest time with those changes. When Bev and I agreed it would be sweet to have our family together for dinner every Friday evening to welcome the Sabbath and to make a break from the busy-ness of the week, Leora immediately perceived our intentions as a full-blown mortar attack on the social life that buzzes right at the center of her fourteen-year-old universe. She fussed and yelled even more than I expected she would, but when eventually she realized that we weren't going to yield, and the battle subsided, she was able to voice what had really got her going. She was afraid, she said, that Friday night dinners would be just the first step on a long road of restrictions, and that ultimately we'd also be ordering her to wear long skirts and never talk to boys.

Let's just do Friday evening dinners and we'll see what that's like for us, we reassured her. It took only a couple of months for her to stop asking if maybe just this Friday she could please, please go to Lindsay's house, and to give up the sour expression on her face over the soup; and though she hasn't said so, I have the clear sense that she, too, now enjoys the space and calm of that one dinner per week where we (and usually a guest or two) eat bountifully and talk leisurely, with about ten times more attention than we usually give each other at any other time in the week.

Leora is not the only one who has felt some ambivalence about bringing the prescriptions and proscriptions of traditional Jewish observance into our lives. Although she's a lot more tolerant than a teenager, Bev hasn't taken much personal interest in becoming more traditional in her Jewish practice. Her strongest source of spiritual energy is her service work as a palliative care physician, which gives her the opportunity to meet others in the place of flowing openness that sometimes erupts when days are numbered and people lose all appetite for life's trivialities or the facades of personality. There have been occasions—such as the time I informed her that the reason I didn't want to fix up a flowerbed one Saturday was because gardening is among the activities traditionally not done on the day of rest—when she has reacted angrily, as if I were just being ridiculous. But I think that, not unlike Leora, she sometimes harbors fears that, as we approach thirty years of marriage, I might be turning into someone she simply won't recognize anymore. Out of love and respect for her, and encouraged by Rabbi Perr, I don't impose any observance on the household that the others don't feel good about for themselves.

It has been surprising that our elder daughter, Julia, who gave every sign of being the freest spirit and the most worldly member of our family, stepped actively into Jewishness as soon as she went away to university. The first Friday she spent in residence, she attended a Sabbath dinner hosted by the university chapter of the Hillel organization. She took Hebrew as one of her freshman courses, and another class on the Holocaust. Still, it's she who gave me the nickname "Chassy" to let it be known that she, too, had doubts and concerns about losing the father she knew to a radical change in life.

My family, it seems, is a pretty conservative lot. Their fear surrounding my newly adopted Jewish behavior is that I will keep on becoming more observant, and that would upset what is otherwise a stable and happy family unit. But they understand that I'm the one who feels the need to keep learning and growing like this, and on balance I have to say that they have all been very supportive and loving of me as I carry on with my journey.

From my point of view, it doesn't feel like they have anything to worry about, even as I do go about trying out new behaviors and seeking change in my life. My secular upbringing and worldly young adulthood are still real factors in who I am, and so I seem to lack some of the basic elements that go into building a strong foundation for an observant life, like unquestioned faith and a commitment to all the rules and regulations, even the ones that make no rational sense. Maybe in time I will feel differently, but from where I stand today, it looks equally possible that I might not. When people ask me where I am with my Judaism now, I answer that I must be a spider, because I seem to have so many feet in different camps. Mine is still an exploration in progress, and I'm staying wide open to whatever might bring more light into my life.

I do go to synagogue more often now. The death of my mother in late 2000 has spurred that along, as it was clear to me that I wanted to do a son's duty by saying the mourner's prayer— the *Kaddish*—on a daily basis. When my father died seven years before, it was equally obvious that I would not be doing that on account of his death. Those differing choices don't reflect anything of my relationship with my two parents, but say a lot about how my relationship to formal ritual has changed in the years between. I don't make a habit of going to any single synagogue, though. I pray around, I say. I've grown to love the tradition; it's just that I haven't found anywhere it's practiced today that works perfectly for me.

No one else in my family has joined me in attending synagogue with any regularity, and I don't try to convince them, because as I see it, that's their choice. I might feel a little differently if I didn't have my own questions about what goes on in Jewish liturgy, but the truth is that I do. The undiluted adulation of the divine that runs through the liturgy gives me the biggest problems, just as the devotional path was never right for my soul when I was exploring Hinduism. I seem not to be endowed with the kind of spirit that is moved and opened up by bowing down and uttering unconditional praise. In America, you might say I'm from Missouri; European Jews would say I was a Litvak (meaning from Lithuania). As it happens, I've never set foot in either Missouri or Lithuania, but, reputedly just like people from those places, I prefer to have at least a little tangible proof or demonstration on which to base my decisions about what to believe and what to do.

I have been able to put aside my issues and continue to go to synagogue regularly, though, by reminding myself how much there is to learn and understand about Jewish liturgy. While I've already learned a lot, I really know very little, and so it's just too early to form any solid judgments, even for myself.

I am also encouraged to continue exploring Jewish prayer because now—as my knowledge of Hebrew and my appreciation for the Mussar perspective grow—there is already more for me in the synagogue service than there ever used to be. To give one example, in the blessings that follow the recitation of the affirmation of God's oneness, the *Shma,* I now read the Hebrew phrase "Put these words of Mine on your heart and on your soul" and hear in that specific choice of words not only an instruction to learn these important teachings so well that they are known "by heart," but also to take on the practice that will inscribe them at the deepest level of soul, so that they become part of the essence of who I am. To me, that means Mussar.

Along the way, I've also developed an appreciation for the traditional Jewish form of learning, which goes on mainly by intensive study of the Talmud. This involves scrutinizing the arguments that are waged right in the Talmudic record and then carried on in subsequent generations by later commentators. More than just learning the facts of who held which opinion, or where the consensus came down, this traditional style of learning demands that the student really enter into the arguments that have been going back and forth through the centuries, in order to come to a personal realization of those things the tradition guides us to consider and understand in our quest for good, wise lives. Text-learning like this appeals to my intellectual training and my personal leanings, and I now meet with a knowledgeable friend once a week for an hour of that sort of study, and have an appetite for more.

I have made no secret of the ambivalence I feel about certain aspects of Jewish practice that are, nevertheless, looming larger in my life these days, but I can say truthfully that I have few of those feelings about Mussar. Mussar has given me a new way to engage with my life that is one part inquiry and one part renovation project. Strands of that discipline have now been implanted in my daily life, where they serve like hidden reinforcement rods that work to shore up and renew the sagging structure of an old building.

I continue to seek out, read, and reread the classic texts of the tradition. Mussar may be an obscure discipline today, but somehow I still haven't come to the end of the books the tradition claims as its own. I'm still catching wind of classics I hadn't yet heard of, and limited-print-run collections of talks given by more recent Mussar teachers. Whenever that happens, I feel as excited as if I'd just glimpsed a beautiful bird that everyone thought might have been extinct. Only the most illustrious of these books have been translated into English, and so I've also been laboring away at improving my Hebrew, no easy task here on the other side of fifty.

Because the emphasis in Rabbi Perr's yeshiva falls on Mussar as a subject of study and reflection more than on its practical exercises, I get especially worked up when I discover in one of these books another of the practices for doing the work of soul-transformation that is Mussar's purpose. That was how I felt when I discovered Rabbi Eliyahu Dessler's guided contemplations, or Rabbi Eliyahu Lopian's report that in the Mussar yeshiva of Kelm before the war the time until midday was set aside as "the period of loyalty," when students were to practice seclusion, divest themselves of all material concerns and troubling thoughts, and strive to concentrate their minds through prayer and study. The afternoon was then given over to the more social "period of service."

As I work my way through old books like these, I'm on the lookout for ideas I can put to work in my own life, and when I come upon teachings about the soul and its journey, I try to see how my own soul-traits, in their present condition, compare to what I find in the sources.

It feels like a gift, to have been awakened to seeing myself as a soul, rather than as just a personality or an ego. I once would have accepted being told I was a soul about as readily as being told I was a Martian, but it is just that view of myself that has now taken firm root. Seeing that I am a soul seems a very accurate description of my inner life, incorporating as it does an unsegmented wholeness of mind and emotions, reason and wisdom. And while the best I can do to make sense of ideas like the endurance of the soul after death, or the resurrection of the dead, is to hang a big question mark after them, I'm forced to consider that, if in the last century we've come to see it as self-evident that energy and matter are conserved in the universe despite changes of form, in the next century we might well come to understand that consciousness is its own category of substance—and that it, too, gets conserved despite the transformation of receptacle. Maybe. Maybe that's what the tradition has been telling us.

The one big question people always seem to ask me when they find out I've been exploring a spiritual discipline is how I've changed since Mussar came into my life. The shortest answer I can give is that I now don't make as many messes as I used to. That's enough good to leave most people nodding appreciatively, especially if they knew me before, but in reality that response begs even more questions than it answers.

I was stewing in pain when I opened up this new chapter in my life, and one of the first changes Mussar helped me make was to accept that my fall didn't have to be terminal. From the point of view of the Mussar masters, it wasn't so surprising that I had taken a tumble, because why should I expect myself to be any more perfect than any of the rest of us? The one time I shared with Rabbi Perr the outline of what had happened in the failure of my business, and especially the stupid and misguided things I had done to precipitate it, he didn't ask for details or probe with questions. He just listened, deeply and quietly, without reacting. And when I had finished, he turned his eyes upward and pursed his lips; then, after a moment, he said quietly, "I've done things that I am ashamed of, too."

That's all he said. He didn't counsel me, or lecture me on my faulty soul-traits or the wiles of the *yetzer ha-ra*. He just joined himself to me, where I was, and made himself my companion. At that cherished moment, he made me feel that we were just two imperfect people, trying to accept our imperfection and to reach out for something more.

Mussar's map of life reassured me, because it has as its starting point the premise that no matter how wonderful, no matter how otherwise stunning, in some way we're all flawed. And yet, at the same time that it has helped me to accept the "basket of worms and bugs" I carry on my back, as the Talmud calls our unsavory personal history, Mussar has also shown me that I am not consigned to the pit, and it directs me to look up toward the peak to which I can aspire. That suggestion has given me hope, because it confirms what I have continued to feel all along: that implanted within me and all of us is the dream and also the possibility of perfection, and the urge to walk a road that carries us higher and higher, and closer to achieving it.

Every day now I do formal Mussar practice. I read and consider some teaching from one of the Mussar classics. I also do the *heshbon ha-nefesh* practice, which has me repeating an affirmation every morning focused on a specific soul-trait, and then in the evening recording the things I have thought or said or done that day that relate to the specific *middah* I am targeting. I do sitting meditation practice in the morning, just as I did when I was active in Buddhist meditation, and right now the meditation I do still owes more to my Buddhist training than to any other source. But that creates no conflict with either Mussar or Judaism, because the meditation I do involves simply holding my awareness on the in-and-out flow of the breath. Doing that sounds a lot easier than it is in reality, because it takes practice to keep attention focused on a single object like breath. But when that ability is developed, it works to empty the mind and hew out one-pointed concentration from amid the noisy chatter that usually occupies the inner terrain.

And then, periodically, I do a retreat. I'll go away somewhere quiet for a day or a weekend, or I'll just stay at home but disengage from my ordinary activities, and on those occasions I intensify my introspection with more meditation, guided contemplations, and chanting.

In refurbishing my life, I have set fixed and regular times for meditation, study, and prayer, as Mussar prescribes. I've done this because I've seen that the sharpened awareness that is fundamental to a life of ascent comes incrementally through consistent practice of introspection and reflection, while the lasting transformation of soul-traits happens only through continuous effort and training.

But these formal practices don't come close to representing the whole of the influence Mussar has had on my life. In fact, because the real workshop for soul-transformation is open to us twenty-four hours a day, the most profound ways that Mussar has infiltrated my life have been informal. It's an outcome of my Mussar practice that I'm constantly more aware of my own thoughts, words, and deeds, as if I'd installed fresh batteries in my inner lamp. I watch myself much more closely in every context, because I now understand that every single thing that passes through my mind or leaves my mouth or is the work of my hand deposits its trace or residue *in me;* and I have become deeply committed to being as selective as possible about how I color and shape the soul that I feel is the primary gift life has bestowed on me.

And, bottom line, what effect has all this learning and practice had? I can only answer provisionally at this point, because I'm able to report back just from the flank of the mountain and not the summit; my engagement with Mussar and the reworking of my life is a journey that is far from over, if it ever will be. I'm aware of the benefits that have come into my life, and as I open up to share them here, it is with the all-important proviso that I am describing only improvements I have seen, not goals I have reached. Mussar tells us we can become whole and even perfect, and while I know I've made progress, I've still got a long, long way to go before I achieve anything that might be called completion.

Right now, my every day is infused with infinitely more gratitude than I had ever known. The gnawing hunger of ambition and ego that had become the driving force in my life has now yielded to a deeper sense of appreciation for the remarkable beneficence that flows through the world. Ironically, I also have a clearer perspective on the problems, ignorance, and evil that are everpresent all around us, but I now see these in truthful proportion to the good that is in the world. I am grateful for consciousness and growth, for companionship and love, for the inspiration and the legacy of all the generations that have come before—and, yes, even for the problems that provide the grit I sometimes need to keep on the path of growing.

If I can continue to grow without actually getting clobbered, I'm doubly appreciative. Rabbi Perr told a story—surprisingly, about a Zen master and his pupil—that made just this point.

"I don't know much about this Zen," he started out, making me cringe a little at what might be coming next. Then he went on: "Every day this pupil came to the master to learn, and the master assigned him to wash dishes. Over the days that followed, at random moments, the master would sneak up on the student and hit him over the head with a stick. Just like that. Then one day, as he was washing dishes, the pupil suddenly had a sense of something coming. He ducked just as the stick whizzed by his head." Rabbi Perr paused for a moment before he explained, "That's what we are doing, too. We're developing an awareness of what you can only sense, not see with your eyes or feel with your hands." His eyes twinkled like fireflies glowing between the dark sky of his hat and the thicket of his beard. "Sometimes, you know, I wish we also had a tradition of hitting the student over the head with a stick, because I'm not always sure how much of this is penetrating!" And then he laughed warmly as I considered how grateful I feel whenever I am able to "take a lesson" without needing that sort of stimulus.

There is even room in my gratitude for sadness and grief. They're part of living too, and I can see that without the "seasoning" that comes from the dark side of life, we will more likely turn out to be bland and shallow people. My own experience has led me to appreciate the transformative, softening power of a broken heart, and I now feel a natural compassion that enables me to support and encourage others in their pain, because I've learned that there's nothing quite like tears to bring out the deep, effulgent radiance that is our potential.

I feel as if I've been healing from the fall I took and also growing into a deeper way of living. Maybe in time that process will carry me beyond the exploration of grief and loss, even into the territory of joy. I'd be up for that.

Since my first introduction to spirituality and things Eastern, I've understood that self-awareness is the fundamental quality to be cultivated in a spiritual life. It's hard for me to separate the effect of all the meditation I've done, dating back to 1974, from what can be attributed specifically to Mussar, but I am certain that I continue to become more self-aware in my life. And although my awareness is still something less than diamond-clear, I am committed to working at it because I appreciate the incontestable role that clear inner vision has played in helping me change the way I lead my life, and especially in guiding me to make fewer messes.

The whole Mussar structure rests on telling us that we all have much more free will than we realize, and that only by developing our capacity to choose freely can we hope to trace the best possible path through life. As my own inner awareness has become more clarified, I see how entirely true this is. Whenever I succeed in liberating myself from the grip of wrongdoing or habit even by a tiny increment, by that same degree I increase my ability to exercise choice. And that makes me better able to side-step the potholes and avoid the swinging branches that used to trip me up. I can't will myself to have more free will as long as I am governed by unconscious drives, appetites, and habits. But what I can do is follow the Mussar practice that brings the stuff of the unconscious to consciousness, that makes me more aware of my desires, helps me harness them, and gradually releases me from the grip of ingrained habit.

One thing I have been able to choose has been to increase the stillness in my life. I don't need to fill up my life or my head with action and people, because being alone and quiet is just fine, too. And with that appreciation for stillness has also come more tolerance for mystery, which means that I am more comfortable accepting the fact that there are some things I just don't know or understand—take "God" as a good case in point. And while I won't give up trying to grasp what I can of these things, I know that I might never reach a point of solid understanding, and that'll be okay, too.

Veined through all this change is the fact that I am now softer-hearted than I used to be. Pain has taught me to care more for the pain of others, while the teaching I have received that has allowed me to accept my own imperfection has bred compassion for the particular hands others may have been dealt. I'm still prone to slip into being judgmental or dismissive, but now I also carry around a different perspective, and when I stand in that place, I simply marvel at the tapestry of soul-traits each of us happens to have.

I rarely lose my temper anymore, though I used to more often than I care to admit. Playfulness, as well as tears, is closer to the surface. But, despite these signs of softening, I haven't softened on myself. If anything, with the pain brought on by transgression still fresh in my memory, and my new realization of the truth of my potential to elevate myself (a potential we all have), I don't have any appetite for being too easy or gentle on my own failings. Still, when I come back to consciousness after a gloopy slide down some slippery slope, I'm usually able to pick myself up, make amends, and then resume the climb. I just don't see the value in self-condemnation.

There's a connection between how I view both my enduring weaknesses and my efforts to raise myself up, and the way I now view life itself, especially as I participate in it. It may not have been very apparent, but in hindsight I can see clearly that I used to be frightened of life—no doubt another wound I inherited from my parents, whose worldview was formed by anti-Semitism in Europe, two world wars, and the Great Depression. That deep-seated fear of loss and deprivation that came to me as unconscious baggage, shipped down through the last century, revealed itself in my insatiable drive to make something of myself, as if with my own two hands I could stave off all the dangerous forces of the universe.

Only when I realized how pervasive was this fear could I appreciate the grim humor in the joke that asks why Jews have always been such extraordinary virtuosi at the clarinet and violin, but not the organ. The answer goes that you can't run with an organ. And so I understand why, among all the Mussar teachings, what they had to say about *bitahon*—trust—spoke to so deep a place in me. Having learned those teachings so well that they now kick in almost automatically whenever I feel myself clench up over something that might be about to happen, I have begun to relax into trusting that there is a grander scheme at work in life than what my limited intellect may be able to perceive. And that enhanced trust has given me more confidence to rely on my own inner guidance, and to move forward in my life.

Those are some of the key changes I can trace back to my Mussar learning and practice. I've also found a new and compelling rationale for engaging in social issues, not just to make a measurable difference *out there* but because I now see that I will be less fully human *in here* if I don't make the fullest contribu-

tion I can; this too is a dimension of working on myself. I've been putting some effort into environmental issues, and I carry on with my Mussar practice during committee meetings and at the copy-shop, too.

As I have learned about Mussar and brought its teachings to life in my own experience, opportunities have arisen for me to share what I have learned with others. I had set out only with hopes of finding healing and guidance for my own life, but having discovered in Mussar both a path and a little more light to see by, and because of my academic background, sharing what I've found seems to have been an inevitable progression. When I was given my first opportunity to see my name in print beside the title of a course with the word "Mussar" in it, I immediately asked Rabbi Perr what he thought about my telling others the tale of my journey and what I had learned. "Yes, go ahead," he answered without hesitation, "you'll learn a lot." And I've heard the same thing from him in several discussions since. It's part of his theory of learning that you should try to teach what you've learned, even while you're still learning, because it will show you how much you really do or don't understand, and will likely bring up questions you hadn't yet thought to ask. That's been my experience, too.

I haven't done much Mussar teaching yet, but it has been enough to confirm that the tradition is rich with the kind of wisdom that can meet the spiritual needs of people today—especially Jews and non-Jews who want to develop a transformative personal practice. And yet, in order for the greatest number of people to be able to make the most of Mussar, the tradition has to be reinterpreted in modern terms. Many of the classic Mussar stories tell of wagons breaking down and candles burning out, quaint images that would have been immediately recognizable in

the nineteenth century, but now need to be translated for a world of car and computer crashes and light bulbs expiring. Mussar has been updated in every generation, and so I have hope that people who are more knowledgeable in the tradition than I am will join me in this task.

One other thing I've taken from the teaching I've done is a profound appreciation for the spiritual hunger I see all around me. While we are the recipients, for better or worse, of enormous technological progress and affluence, a dire poverty of wisdom and spirit stalks the land. Empty and hurting souls call out, and a distorted culture responds with invitations to shop at the mall or swear allegiance to professional sports franchises. Starving spirits want to be nourished, and are as vulnerable to the merchants of consumption as they are to hucksters of the heart. For me, it is both an honor and a responsibility to be conveying a tradition that, having been around the track a few times in its thousand years, is truly devoted only to their benefit and the healing of the world.

My exposure to the Eastern traditions seeded in me a notion that death was not the only way to end the struggle of this life, but that Enlightenment or Nirvana were sublime steady states of supreme peace that could be attained right here on earth. Now I see things differently, and I no longer expect that the struggle will end. My expectations changed right back there at the beginning, when I read the words of Rabbi Israel Salanter that leapt out at me from the first article on Mussar I ever laid eyes on: "As long as one lives a life of calmness and tranquility in the service of God, it is clear that he is remote from true service . . ."

Maybe I'm perverse, but I love that teaching, because it warns me that if I find the struggle ending, it might just mean I've

fallen asleep again. Instead of encouraging me to seek escape from the contending, even paradoxical, challenges life keeps throwing at me, Salanter's words guide me to value the struggles I engage in every day. I hear him telling me to find in each and every challenge an opportunity for growth—starting now.

The farther I've traveled on the Mussar path, the more numerous and subtle these challenges have become. The distinctions get finer and finer and the tests more exacting. There is no shortcut. All I can do is take the next step, and the step after that. If Salanter is right, all the climbing will not lead to some internal Eden of the soul here on earth, but even if it doesn't, I've come to understand that the climb's the thing. Living a life of ascent, not necessarily reaching the peak, is what I've found as an answer to my life's question.

In Hebrew, the word for steps is *ma'alot*. The same word also means "virtue." Mussar makes something of this. Virtue is not a distant goal we strive for, it is the quality we bring into every one of the steps we take as we walk the path of ascent.

"You just keep going," Rabbi Perr told us in a *shmooze* one day, his grave face swiveling slowly to take in every being in the room and make contact with every pair of eyes, "and you can get there. Even if you know yourself to be a *shnook,* you shouldn't give up. You may be a *shnook,*" he shrugged, "but you shouldn't give up. There is hope. And you can do something about yourself; you needn't remain a *shnook.*" And then he added, "And by the way, every one of us is a *shnook.* It's just—welcome to the club." And he smiled knowingly.

Change has come slowly, and hasn't always been evident to me. I've drawn encouragement from the Mussar teachers who have trod this way before me, such as Rabbi Salanter, who says,

"Do not be discouraged if your study of Mussar does not seem to produce results. If your study seems to make no impression at all on your soul, if your ways seem not to have changed at all, know with true faith that even if success is not revealed to the eyes of your body, it is revealed to the eyes of your mind. As you learn Mussar more and more, the hidden impressions it makes upon you gather together and have an effect."

I rely on that encouragement because it tells me that spiritual practice transforms, even if I can't see the changes, just as a tree grows even if we don't perceive the growth.

Whether or not we ourselves see the effects, in the end we are all naturally endowed with the possibility for change and improvement. Rabbi Perr believes this too. "I still believe people are good," he told me one day. "I believe you can talk to people about the truth, and that people would like to raise themselves out of the morass of their lives. I believe they feel better when they try to improve, and that there is such a thing as making better people. I believe you do become better by working at it, and that it is our job to teach these things and to make people better—for their sake, for the sake of society, for the sake of the Torah, and for the sake of everything that is precious in the world that gives meaning to life. It has to be done."

And how is it done? So far, what I've learned is to study the Mussar texts, do the practices, seek out teachers like Rabbi Perr who embody one thousand years of hard-won human experience, and to draw upon the lessons I find in my own life. Mussar guides me. It says: *Look! See! Hear! The message is right there, in the world around you.* And once I have received that message, I can begin to write a revised text for my life by exercising free

will and responding to the trustworthy little voice that whispers from within.

In fact, the deepest message of all is actually written between the lines; and that brings to mind one final story I'd like to share.

There was once a wise man who claimed he could read the white spaces on the parchment of the Torah. He declared that he had a secret ability to decipher the spaces between the letters, and between the written lines, and in the margins. People challenged him on this claim, and one day he said he would reveal what the white spaces said. The doubters should come to his house, he would entertain them with hospitality, and in time he would reveal what he knew.

People came to his house. They enjoyed food, and they drank sociably. The evening wore on, and then someone asked, "So, tell us. What do the white spaces say?" The man told his guests to be patient, to eat, to drink, and in due time he would speak.

They ate and they drank, and the evening turned to night, and still no teaching was forthcoming.

It was past midnight when they finally became impatient. "Come on," they insisted, "tell us already."

"All right," the man said. "I'll tell you everything it says between the letters and between the lines and in the margins of the Torah."

The room hushed in anticipation. The man paused, and then he said: "It says: 'Don't be a cockroach!'"

Which says to me that behind the text is a simple message: be a *mensch*. I say to myself: be as fine as you can be.

ALAN MORINIS was born in Toronto. He completed his doctorate in social anthropology at Oxford University, which he attended on a Rhodes Scholarship. The founder and director of the Mussar Institute, he is also the author of *Everyday Holiness: The Jewish Spiritual Path of Mussar.*

Alan has held posts at several universities, and has been a founder and director of nonprofit organizations, including the Seva Foundation and Adam va-Adamah Environmental Society. He has produced award-winning feature films, documentaries, and television programs. He lives in Vancouver, British Columbia, with his wife of thirty years, Dr. Bev Spring, and their two daughters, Julia and Leora.

You can reach Alan Morinis by e-mail at *alan@mussarinstitute.org.* His website to support the learning and teaching of Mussar is located at *www.mussarinstitute.org.*